87 Meat Recipes for Home

By: Kelly Johnson

Table of Contents

Chicken Recipes:
- Roasted Chicken with Lemon and Garlic
- Chicken Parmesan
- Chicken Alfredo Pasta
- Grilled Chicken Skewers with Tzatziki Sauce
- Chicken Piccata
- Chicken Fajitas
- BBQ Chicken Wings
- Chicken and Mushroom Risotto
- Chicken Tikka Masala
- Chicken Pot Pie
- Chicken Caesar Salad
- CHicken and Broccoli Stir-Fry
- Buffalo Chicken Dip

Beef Recipes:
- Beef Stroganoff
- Beef Tacos
- Classic Beef Burger
- Beef and Broccoli
- Beef Chili
- Spaghetti Bolognese
- Beef Kabobs with Chimichurri Sauce
- Beef Enchiladas
- Beef and Vegetable Stir-Fry
- Beef and Guinness Stew
- Sloppy Joes
- Philly Cheesesteak Sandwich
- Korean BBQ Beef
- Beef Satay Skewers

Pork Recipes:
- Pulled Pork Sandwiches
- Pork Tenderloin with Apple Cider Glaze
- Pork Chops with Dijon Mustard Sauce
- Cuban Mojo Pork

- Pork Carnitas Tacos
- Honey Mustard Glazed Ham
- Pork and Pineapple Skewers
- BBQ Pulled Pork Pizza
- Pork Stir-Fry with Vegetables
- Sausage and Peppers
- Pork and Bean Casserole
- Maple Glazed Pork Belly

Lamb Recipes:

- Grilled Lamb Chops with Mint Pesto
- Lamb Gyros
- Moroccan Lamb Tagine
- Lamb Kofta
- Shepherd's Pie with Lamb
- Rack of Lamb with Rosemary and Garlic
- Lamb and Lentil Soup
- Greek Lamb Souvlaki
- Lamb Shank Stew
- Lamb Curry

Turkey Recipes:

- Thanksgiving Roast Turkey
- Turkey Meatballs
- Turkey and Cranberry Panini
- Ground Turkey Chili
- Turkey and Avocado Wrap
- Turkey Pot Pie
- Turkey Tetrazzini
- Grilled Turkey Burgers
- Turkey and Vegetable Skewers
- Turkey Lasagna

Seafood Recipes:

- Grilled Shrimp Skewers
- Lemon Garlic Butter Salmon
- Shrimp Scampi
- Crab Cakes
- Fish Tacos with Chipotle Mayo
- Baked Cod with Herbs

- Garlic Butter Lobster Tails
- Clam Linguine
- Seafood Paella
- Teriyaki Glazed Grilled Swordfish

Miscellaneous Meat Recipes:
- Meatball Subs
- Stuffed Bell Peppers with Ground Meat
- Meat Lover's Pizza
- Empanadas with Ground Meat
- Beef and Sausage Lasagna
- Kebabs with Mixed Meats
- Meat and Cheese Platter
- Meat Pie
- Chili Con Carne
- Carnitas Burritos
- Meat and Potato Casserole
- Meatloaf with Tomato Glaze
- Greek Moussaka
- Tandoori Chicken Pizza
- Italian Sausage and Peppers Calzone
- Bacon-Wrapped Meatloaf
- Meaty Baked Ziti

Chicken Recipe:
Roasted Chicken with Lemon and Garlic

Ingredients:

- 1 whole chicken (about 3-4 pounds)
- Salt and pepper, to taste
- 2 lemons, sliced
- 1 head of garlic, halved horizontally
- 2 tablespoons olive oil
- 1 teaspoon dried thyme
- 1 teaspoon dried rosemary
- 1 teaspoon paprika
- 1 cup chicken broth

Instructions:

Preheat your oven to 425°F (220°C).

Rinse the chicken inside and out, then pat it dry with paper towels. Season the chicken generously with salt and pepper, both inside and outside.

Place the chicken in a roasting pan, breast side up.

In a small bowl, mix together the olive oil, dried thyme, dried rosemary, and paprika to create a seasoning paste.

Rub the seasoning paste all over the chicken, ensuring an even coating.

Stuff the cavity of the chicken with lemon slices and garlic halves.

Place the remaining lemon slices and garlic halves around the chicken in the roasting pan.

Pour the chicken broth into the bottom of the pan.

Roast the chicken in the preheated oven for about 1 hour and 15 minutes or until the internal temperature reaches 165°F (74°C) and the skin is golden brown and crispy.

Baste the chicken with the pan juices every 20-30 minutes to keep it moist.

Once done, remove the chicken from the oven and let it rest for about 10 minutes before carving.

Serve the roasted chicken with the lemon and garlic slices, and drizzle some of the pan juices over the top.

Enjoy your delicious Roasted Chicken with Lemon and Garlic!

Chicken Parmesan

Ingredients:

- 4 boneless, skinless chicken breasts
- Salt and black pepper, to taste
- 1 cup all-purpose flour
- 2 large eggs
- 2 cups Italian-style breadcrumbs
- 1 cup grated Parmesan cheese
- Olive oil, for frying
- 2 cups marinara sauce
- 1 1/2 cups shredded mozzarella cheese
- Fresh basil or parsley, for garnish

Instructions:

Preheat the oven to 375°F (190°C).
Season the chicken breasts with salt and pepper.
Set up a breading station with three shallow dishes: one with flour, one with beaten eggs, and one with a mixture of breadcrumbs and grated Parmesan cheese.
Dredge each chicken breast in the flour, shaking off excess. Dip it into the beaten eggs, allowing any excess to drip off. Press the chicken into the breadcrumb and Parmesan mixture, ensuring an even coating.
Heat olive oil in a large skillet over medium-high heat. Fry the breaded chicken breasts for about 3-4 minutes per side or until golden brown and cooked through.
Transfer the cooked chicken to a paper towel-lined plate to drain any excess oil.
In a baking dish, spread a thin layer of marinara sauce. Place the fried chicken breasts on top of the sauce.
Spoon more marinara sauce over each chicken breast, then sprinkle shredded mozzarella cheese on top.
Bake in the preheated oven for 20-25 minutes or until the cheese is melted and bubbly.
Optional: Broil for an additional 1-2 minutes to achieve a golden brown color on the cheese.
Garnish with fresh basil or parsley before serving.

Serve the Chicken Parmesan over pasta or with a side of crusty bread for a satisfying meal.

Enjoy!

Chicken Alfredo Pasta

Ingredients:

- 8 oz (about 225g) fettuccine pasta
- 1 lb (about 450g) boneless, skinless chicken breasts, cut into bite-sized pieces
- Salt and black pepper, to taste
- 2 tablespoons olive oil
- 4 cloves garlic, minced
- 1 cup heavy cream
- 1 cup grated Parmesan cheese
- 1/2 cup unsalted butter
- Fresh parsley, chopped, for garnish

Instructions:

Cook the fettuccine pasta according to the package instructions in a large pot of salted boiling water. Drain and set aside.

Season the chicken pieces with salt and pepper.

In a large skillet, heat olive oil over medium-high heat. Add the chicken and cook until browned and cooked through, about 5-7 minutes. Remove the chicken from the skillet and set aside.

In the same skillet, add minced garlic and sauté for about 1 minute until fragrant.

Reduce the heat to medium-low, then add the heavy cream, butter, and grated Parmesan cheese to the skillet. Stir continuously until the cheese is melted and the sauce is smooth and creamy.

Return the cooked chicken to the skillet, stirring to coat it with the Alfredo sauce. Cook for an additional 2-3 minutes until the chicken is heated through.

Add the cooked fettuccine pasta to the skillet, tossing to coat the pasta evenly with the Alfredo sauce.

Season with additional salt and pepper to taste.

Serve the Chicken Alfredo Pasta in bowls, garnished with chopped fresh parsley.

Enjoy this rich and comforting Chicken Alfredo Pasta as a delightful main course!

Grilled Chicken Skewers with Tzatziki Sauce

Ingredients:

- 1.5 lbs (about 700g) boneless, skinless chicken breasts, cut into bite-sized pieces
- 2 tablespoons olive oil
- 2 cloves garlic, minced
- 1 teaspoon dried oregano
- 1 teaspoon dried thyme
- 1 teaspoon paprika
- Salt and black pepper, to taste
- Wooden skewers (pre-soaked in water for at least 30 minutes)

Instructions:

In a bowl, combine olive oil, minced garlic, dried oregano, dried thyme, paprika, salt, and black pepper to create the marinade.

Add the chicken pieces to the marinade, ensuring they are well-coated. Cover and refrigerate for at least 30 minutes to let the flavors meld.

Preheat the grill to medium-high heat.

Thread the marinated chicken pieces onto the pre-soaked wooden skewers.

Grill the chicken skewers for about 5-7 minutes per side or until fully cooked and slightly charred.

Remove the skewers from the grill and let them rest for a few minutes.

Tzatziki Sauce:

Ingredients:

- 1 cup Greek yogurt
- 1 cucumber, grated and squeezed to remove excess water
- 2 cloves garlic, minced
- 1 tablespoon fresh dill, chopped
- 1 tablespoon fresh mint, chopped
- 1 tablespoon lemon juice
- Salt and black pepper, to taste

Instructions:

In a bowl, combine Greek yogurt, grated cucumber, minced garlic, chopped dill, chopped mint, lemon juice, salt, and black pepper.

Mix well until all ingredients are thoroughly combined.

Refrigerate the Tzatziki sauce for at least 30 minutes to allow the flavors to meld.

Serving:

Serve the Grilled Chicken Skewers with a side of Tzatziki Sauce for dipping. Garnish with additional fresh herbs if desired. This dish pairs well with pita bread or a Greek salad for a complete and delightful meal!

Chicken Piccata

Ingredients:

- 4 boneless, skinless chicken breasts
- Salt and black pepper, to taste
- 1 cup all-purpose flour, for dredging
- 4 tablespoons unsalted butter
- 2 tablespoons olive oil
- 1/2 cup chicken broth
- 1/3 cup fresh lemon juice (about 2 lemons)
- 1/4 cup capers, drained
- 1/4 cup fresh parsley, chopped, for garnish
- Lemon slices, for garnish

Instructions:

Prep the Chicken:
- Pat the chicken breasts dry with paper towels.
- Season both sides with salt and black pepper.
- Dredge the chicken in flour, shaking off any excess.

Cook the Chicken:
- In a large skillet, heat 2 tablespoons of butter and olive oil over medium-high heat.
- Add the chicken breasts and cook for about 3-4 minutes per side or until golden brown and cooked through.
- Remove the chicken from the skillet and set aside.

Prepare the Sauce:
- In the same skillet, add the chicken broth, lemon juice, capers, and the remaining 2 tablespoons of butter.
- Stir and scrape the browned bits from the bottom of the pan.
- Let the sauce simmer for 2-3 minutes to reduce slightly.

Finish Cooking:
- Return the cooked chicken to the skillet, allowing it to heat through and soak up the flavors of the sauce.

Serve:
- Plate the chicken, spoon the sauce over the top, and garnish with chopped parsley and lemon slices.

Optional:
- Serve the Chicken Piccata over cooked pasta, rice, or with a side of vegetables.

Enjoy your Chicken Piccata with its bright and zesty flavors! It's a perfect dish for a quick and elegant dinner.

Chicken Fajitas

Ingredients:

For the Chicken Marinade:

- 1.5 lbs (about 700g) boneless, skinless chicken breasts, sliced into thin strips
- 3 tablespoons olive oil
- 2 tablespoons lime juice
- 2 cloves garlic, minced
- 1 teaspoon chili powder
- 1 teaspoon cumin
- 1 teaspoon paprika
- 1 teaspoon onion powder
- 1/2 teaspoon oregano
- Salt and black pepper, to taste

For the Fajitas:

- 1 large onion, thinly sliced
- 1 large bell pepper (any color), thinly sliced
- 1 tablespoon vegetable oil
- Flour tortillas
- Optional toppings: salsa, guacamole, sour cream, shredded cheese, chopped cilantro, lime wedges

Instructions:

Marinate the Chicken:
- In a bowl, combine olive oil, lime juice, minced garlic, chili powder, cumin, paprika, onion powder, oregano, salt, and black pepper to create the marinade.
- Add the sliced chicken to the marinade, making sure each piece is well-coated. Marinate for at least 30 minutes, or refrigerate for up to 4 hours.

Cook the Chicken:
- Heat a large skillet or grill pan over medium-high heat.
- Add the marinated chicken slices and cook for 3-4 minutes per side or until cooked through and slightly charred.
- Remove the chicken from the skillet and set aside.

Cook the Vegetables:
- In the same skillet, add 1 tablespoon of vegetable oil.
- Add the sliced onions and bell peppers. Cook for 5-7 minutes or until the vegetables are softened and slightly caramelized.

Combine and Serve:
- Return the cooked chicken to the skillet with the vegetables. Toss everything together for a minute or two until well combined and heated through.

Warm the Tortillas:
- Heat the flour tortillas in a dry skillet or microwave according to package instructions.

Assemble the Fajitas:
- Spoon the chicken and vegetable mixture onto warm tortillas.
- Add your choice of toppings, such as salsa, guacamole, sour cream, shredded cheese, chopped cilantro, and a squeeze of lime.

Serve immediately and enjoy your Chicken Fajitas!

These fajitas are perfect for a quick and satisfying weeknight dinner or a casual gathering with friends and family.

BBQ Chicken Wings

Ingredients:

- 2 lbs (about 1 kg) chicken wings, split at joints, tips discarded
- Salt and black pepper, to taste
- 1 teaspoon garlic powder
- 1 teaspoon onion powder
- 1 teaspoon smoked paprika
- 1 cup barbecue sauce (store-bought or homemade)
- 2 tablespoons olive oil
- Optional: Celery sticks and ranch or blue cheese dressing for serving

Instructions:

Preheat the Oven:
- Preheat your oven to 400°F (200°C).

Prepare the Chicken Wings:
- Pat the chicken wings dry with paper towels to remove excess moisture.
- Season the wings with salt, black pepper, garlic powder, onion powder, and smoked paprika. Toss to coat evenly.

Bake the Chicken Wings:
- Place a wire rack on a baking sheet to allow air circulation around the wings.
- Arrange the seasoned chicken wings on the rack.
- Bake in the preheated oven for about 45-50 minutes or until the wings are golden brown and crispy, turning them halfway through the cooking time.

Prepare the BBQ Sauce:
- While the wings are baking, heat olive oil in a saucepan over medium heat.
- Add the barbecue sauce and warm it through. You can also add a bit of extra flavor by incorporating a splash of hot sauce or a squeeze of lime, if desired.

Coat the Wings:
- Once the wings are cooked, transfer them to a large bowl.
- Pour the warmed barbecue sauce over the wings and toss to coat them evenly.

Serve:
- Arrange the BBQ-coated wings on a serving platter.
- Optionally, serve with celery sticks and a side of ranch or blue cheese dressing for dipping.

Enjoy your BBQ Chicken Wings!

These wings are great for sharing and are sure to be a hit at any gathering. Adjust the spice level and sauce quantity according to your preferences.

Chicken and Mushroom Risotto

Ingredients:

- 1.5 lbs (about 700g) boneless, skinless chicken breasts, cut into bite-sized pieces
- Salt and black pepper, to taste
- 2 tablespoons olive oil
- 1 onion, finely chopped
- 2 cloves garlic, minced
- 1 cup Arborio rice
- 1/2 cup dry white wine (optional)
- 8 oz (about 225g) mushrooms, sliced
- 4 cups chicken broth, kept warm
- 1 cup Parmesan cheese, grated
- 1/2 cup heavy cream
- 2 tablespoons butter
- Fresh parsley, chopped, for garnish

Instructions:

Cook the Chicken:
- Season the chicken pieces with salt and black pepper.
- In a large skillet or a wide, shallow pan, heat 1 tablespoon of olive oil over medium-high heat.
- Add the chicken pieces and cook until browned and cooked through. Remove from the pan and set aside.

Sauté Onion and Garlic:
- In the same pan, add another tablespoon of olive oil.
- Add the finely chopped onion and cook until softened.
- Add the minced garlic and sauté for an additional 1-2 minutes until fragrant.

Cook the Mushrooms:
- Add the sliced mushrooms to the pan and cook until they release their moisture and become golden brown.

Toast the Rice:
- Stir in the Arborio rice and cook for 1-2 minutes, allowing the rice to toast slightly.

Deglaze with Wine (Optional):
- Pour in the white wine, if using, and stir until the liquid is mostly absorbed.

Add Broth Gradually:
- Begin adding the warm chicken broth to the rice one ladle at a time.
- Stir constantly and allow the liquid to be absorbed before adding the next ladle.
- Continue this process until the rice is creamy and cooked al dente. This should take about 18-20 minutes.

Finish the Risotto:
- Stir in the cooked chicken, grated Parmesan cheese, heavy cream, and butter.
- Season with additional salt and pepper to taste.

Serve:
- Garnish with chopped fresh parsley and serve the Chicken and Mushroom Risotto hot.

Enjoy this rich and satisfying Chicken and Mushroom Risotto as a comforting main dish!

Chicken Tikka Masala

Ingredients:

For the Chicken Marinade:

- 1.5 lbs (about 700g) boneless, skinless chicken thighs or breasts, cut into bite-sized pieces
- 1 cup plain yogurt
- 2 tablespoons ginger-garlic paste
- 1 teaspoon ground turmeric
- 1 teaspoon ground cumin
- 1 teaspoon ground coriander
- 1 teaspoon chili powder
- 1 teaspoon smoked paprika
- Salt and black pepper, to taste
- 2 tablespoons vegetable oil

For the Tikka Masala Sauce:

- 2 tablespoons vegetable oil
- 1 large onion, finely chopped
- 2 cloves garlic, minced
- 1 tablespoon ginger, grated
- 1 teaspoon ground cumin
- 1 teaspoon ground coriander
- 1 teaspoon garam masala
- 1 teaspoon chili powder
- 1 teaspoon turmeric
- 1 can (14 oz) crushed tomatoes
- 1 cup heavy cream
- Salt, to taste
- Fresh cilantro, chopped, for garnish
- Cooked basmati rice, for serving

Instructions:

Marinate the Chicken:
- In a bowl, combine yogurt, ginger-garlic paste, ground turmeric, ground cumin, ground coriander, chili powder, smoked paprika, salt, and black pepper.

- Add the chicken pieces to the marinade, making sure they are well-coated. Marinate for at least 2 hours, or overnight in the refrigerator.

Grill or Bake the Chicken:
- Preheat your grill or oven to high heat.
- Thread the marinated chicken pieces onto skewers.
- Grill or bake the chicken until fully cooked and slightly charred, about 15-20 minutes.

Prepare the Tikka Masala Sauce:
- In a large skillet, heat vegetable oil over medium heat.
- Add chopped onions and sauté until translucent.
- Add minced garlic and grated ginger, cooking for an additional 1-2 minutes.

Spice Blend:
- Stir in ground cumin, ground coriander, garam masala, chili powder, and turmeric. Cook for 1-2 minutes until the spices are fragrant.

Add Tomatoes and Cream:
- Pour in the crushed tomatoes, stirring well to combine.
- Add the grilled or baked chicken to the skillet.
- Pour in the heavy cream and simmer for 10-15 minutes, allowing the flavors to meld.

Season and Garnish:
- Season with salt to taste.
- Garnish with chopped fresh cilantro.

Serve:
- Serve the Chicken Tikka Masala over cooked basmati rice.

Enjoy the rich and flavorful Chicken Tikka Masala with its aromatic spices and creamy tomato sauce!

Chicken Pot Pie

Ingredients:

For the Filling:

- 2 cups cooked chicken, shredded or diced
- 2 tablespoons unsalted butter
- 1 onion, finely chopped
- 2 carrots, diced
- 2 celery stalks, diced
- 1 cup frozen peas
- 1/3 cup all-purpose flour
- 1/2 teaspoon dried thyme
- 1/2 teaspoon dried rosemary
- 1/2 teaspoon dried sage
- Salt and black pepper, to taste
- 2 cups chicken broth
- 1 cup whole milk or half-and-half

For the Crust:

- 1 package store-bought refrigerated pie crusts (2 crusts) or homemade pie crust

Instructions:

Preheat the Oven:
- Preheat your oven to 425°F (220°C).

Prepare the Filling:
- In a large skillet, melt the butter over medium heat.
- Add chopped onions, carrots, and celery. Cook until the vegetables are softened, about 5-7 minutes.
- Stir in the flour and cook for an additional 1-2 minutes to create a roux.
- Gradually add the chicken broth and milk, stirring constantly to avoid lumps.
- Add the shredded or diced chicken, frozen peas, dried thyme, dried rosemary, dried sage, salt, and black pepper.
- Simmer the mixture until it thickens, about 5-7 minutes. Remove from heat.

Prepare the Crust:
- Roll out one pie crust and place it in the bottom of a 9-inch pie dish.
- Pour the chicken filling into the pie crust.

Top with Crust:
- Roll out the second pie crust and place it over the filling. Seal the edges and crimp them with a fork.
- Optionally, cut a few slits in the top crust to allow steam to escape.

Bake:
- Bake in the preheated oven for 30-35 minutes or until the crust is golden brown.

Cool and Serve:
- Allow the Chicken Pot Pie to cool for a few minutes before slicing and serving.

Enjoy your comforting Chicken Pot Pie, a perfect meal for chilly evenings!

Chicken Caesar Salad

Ingredients:

For the Salad:

- 2 boneless, skinless chicken breasts
- Salt and black pepper, to taste
- 1 tablespoon olive oil
- 1 head romaine lettuce, washed and chopped
- 1 cup cherry tomatoes, halved
- 1/2 cup croutons
- 1/4 cup grated Parmesan cheese

For the Caesar Dressing:

- 1/2 cup mayonnaise
- 2 tablespoons grated Parmesan cheese
- 1 tablespoon Dijon mustard
- 1 tablespoon Worcestershire sauce
- 2 garlic cloves, minced
- 2 tablespoons lemon juice
- Salt and black pepper, to taste

Instructions:

Grill the Chicken:
- Season the chicken breasts with salt and black pepper.
- Heat olive oil in a grill pan or skillet over medium-high heat.
- Grill the chicken breasts for about 5-7 minutes per side or until cooked through.
- Allow the chicken to rest for a few minutes before slicing.

Prepare the Caesar Dressing:
- In a bowl, whisk together mayonnaise, grated Parmesan cheese, Dijon mustard, Worcestershire sauce, minced garlic, lemon juice, salt, and black pepper.
- Adjust the seasoning to taste.

Assemble the Salad:
- In a large salad bowl, toss the chopped romaine lettuce with cherry tomatoes, croutons, and grated Parmesan cheese.

Add Grilled Chicken:

- Slice the grilled chicken breasts and add them to the salad.

Dress the Salad:
- Pour the Caesar dressing over the salad.
- Toss everything together until the salad is well coated with the dressing.

Serve:
- Divide the Chicken Caesar Salad among serving plates.
- Optionally, garnish with extra Parmesan cheese and croutons.

Enjoy your delicious Chicken Caesar Salad!

This salad makes for a satisfying and complete meal, perfect for lunch or a light dinner. The combination of flavors and textures is sure to please your taste buds.

Chicken and Broccoli Stir-Fry

Ingredients:

For the Stir-Fry:

- 1.5 lbs (about 700g) boneless, skinless chicken breasts, thinly sliced
- 3 cups broccoli florets
- 2 tablespoons vegetable oil
- 3 cloves garlic, minced
- 1 teaspoon ginger, grated
- Sesame seeds and sliced green onions for garnish (optional)

For the Sauce:

- 1/4 cup soy sauce
- 2 tablespoons oyster sauce
- 1 tablespoon hoisin sauce
- 1 tablespoon cornstarch
- 1 tablespoon water
- 1 teaspoon sugar
- 1/2 teaspoon sesame oil
- 1/4 teaspoon black pepper

Instructions:

Prepare the Sauce:
- In a small bowl, whisk together soy sauce, oyster sauce, hoisin sauce, cornstarch, water, sugar, sesame oil, and black pepper. Set aside.

Stir-Fry the Chicken:
- Heat 1 tablespoon of vegetable oil in a wok or large skillet over medium-high heat.
- Add sliced chicken and stir-fry until browned and cooked through. Remove the chicken from the pan and set aside.

Stir-Fry the Broccoli:
- In the same pan, add another tablespoon of oil if needed.
- Add minced garlic and grated ginger, and stir-fry for about 30 seconds until fragrant.
- Add broccoli florets and stir-fry for 3-4 minutes until they are tender-crisp.

Combine Chicken and Broccoli:
- Return the cooked chicken to the pan with the broccoli.

Add the Sauce:
- Pour the prepared sauce over the chicken and broccoli.
- Toss everything together until the chicken and broccoli are evenly coated with the sauce.

Finish and Garnish:
- Continue cooking for an additional 1-2 minutes until the sauce thickens.
- Optionally, garnish with sesame seeds and sliced green onions.

Serve:
- Serve the Chicken and Broccoli Stir-Fry over steamed rice or noodles.

Enjoy this flavorful and nutritious Chicken and Broccoli Stir-Fry as a quick and easy weeknight meal!

Buffalo Chicken Dip

Ingredients:

- 2 cups cooked and shredded chicken (rotisserie chicken works well)
- 1/2 cup buffalo sauce (adjust to taste)
- 1/2 cup ranch dressing
- 8 oz (about 225g) cream cheese, softened
- 1 cup shredded cheddar cheese
- 1 cup shredded mozzarella cheese
- 1/4 cup blue cheese crumbles (optional)
- 1/4 cup green onions, chopped (for garnish)
- Tortilla chips, celery sticks, or carrot sticks for serving

Instructions:

Preheat the Oven:
- Preheat your oven to 350°F (175°C).

Prepare the Chicken:
- Cook and shred the chicken. You can use pre-cooked rotisserie chicken or boil and shred chicken breasts.

Mix the Ingredients:
- In a mixing bowl, combine the shredded chicken, buffalo sauce, ranch dressing, softened cream cheese, cheddar cheese, mozzarella cheese, and optional blue cheese crumbles.
- Mix until all ingredients are well combined.

Bake the Dip:
- Transfer the mixture to a baking dish, spreading it evenly.

Bake in the Oven:
- Bake in the preheated oven for 25-30 minutes or until the dip is hot and bubbly.

Garnish:
- Remove the dip from the oven and sprinkle chopped green onions on top for garnish.

Serve:
- Serve the Buffalo Chicken Dip hot with tortilla chips, celery sticks, or carrot sticks for dipping.

Enjoy the creamy and spicy goodness of Buffalo Chicken Dip at your next party or game day gathering! It's sure to be a hit.

Beef Recipes:
Beef Stroganoff

Ingredients:

- 1.5 lbs (about 700g) beef sirloin or tenderloin, thinly sliced into strips
- Salt and black pepper, to taste
- 2 tablespoons olive oil
- 1 onion, finely chopped
- 2 cloves garlic, minced
- 8 oz (about 225g) mushrooms, sliced
- 2 tablespoons all-purpose flour
- 1 cup beef broth
- 2 tablespoons Worcestershire sauce
- 2 tablespoons Dijon mustard
- 1/2 cup sour cream
- 2 tablespoons fresh parsley, chopped
- Cooked egg noodles or rice, for serving

Instructions:

Prepare the Beef:
- Season the beef strips with salt and black pepper.

Sear the Beef:
- Heat olive oil in a large skillet over medium-high heat.
- Add the sliced beef and sear until browned on all sides. Remove the beef from the skillet and set aside.

Sauté Onion and Mushrooms:
- In the same skillet, add chopped onion and sauté until softened.
- Add minced garlic and sliced mushrooms. Cook until the mushrooms release their moisture and become golden brown.

Make the Sauce:
- Sprinkle flour over the mushrooms and stir to coat, cooking for an additional minute.
- Gradually whisk in beef broth, Worcestershire sauce, and Dijon mustard. Bring to a simmer and let it thicken.

Combine Beef and Sauce:
- Return the seared beef to the skillet, allowing it to cook in the sauce for a few minutes.

Finish the Dish:
- Stir in sour cream, ensuring it is well incorporated into the sauce.

- Adjust the seasoning with salt and pepper to taste.

Garnish and Serve:
- Garnish the Beef Stroganoff with chopped fresh parsley.
- Serve over cooked egg noodles or rice.

Enjoy the creamy and savory goodness of Beef Stroganoff for a comforting and satisfying meal!

Beef Tacos

Ingredients:

For the Seasoned Ground Beef:

- 1 lb (about 450g) ground beef
- 1 onion, finely chopped
- 2 cloves garlic, minced
- 1 tablespoon chili powder
- 1 teaspoon ground cumin
- 1 teaspoon paprika
- 1/2 teaspoon dried oregano
- Salt and black pepper, to taste
- 1/2 cup beef broth

For Assembling Tacos:

- Taco shells (hard or soft)
- Shredded lettuce
- Diced tomatoes
- Shredded cheese (cheddar or Mexican blend)
- Sour cream
- Salsa
- Fresh cilantro, chopped
- Lime wedges

Instructions:

Cook the Seasoned Ground Beef:
- In a skillet over medium heat, cook the ground beef until browned, breaking it apart with a spoon as it cooks.
- Drain any excess fat.
- Add chopped onion and minced garlic to the beef, cooking until the onion is softened.

Season the Beef:
- Add chili powder, ground cumin, paprika, dried oregano, salt, and black pepper to the beef mixture. Stir well to combine.
- Pour in beef broth and simmer for 5-7 minutes until the mixture is heated through and the flavors meld.

Assemble the Tacos:

- Warm the taco shells according to package instructions.
- Spoon the seasoned ground beef into the taco shells.

Add Toppings:
- Customize your tacos with your favorite toppings, such as shredded lettuce, diced tomatoes, shredded cheese, sour cream, salsa, and chopped cilantro.

Serve:
- Serve the beef tacos with lime wedges on the side.

Feel free to get creative and add your favorite taco toppings to make them just the way you like! Beef tacos are perfect for a casual and fun family dinner or for entertaining friends.

Classic Beef Burger

Ingredients:

For the Patties:

- 1 pound ground beef (80% lean, 20% fat for juicier burgers)
- Salt and black pepper to taste
- 4 hamburger buns

For Toppings (Optional):

- Cheese slices (cheddar, American, Swiss, or your favorite)
- Lettuce leaves
- Tomato slices
- Onion slices
- Pickles
- Ketchup, mustard, and mayonnaise

Instructions:

Preheat the Grill or Pan:
- If using a grill, preheat it to medium-high heat. If cooking on a stovetop, heat a pan or skillet over medium-high heat.

Shape the Patties:
- Divide the ground beef into four equal portions. Shape each portion into a round patty, making them slightly larger than the buns as they will shrink during cooking.
- Season both sides of each patty with salt and black pepper.

Cook the Patties:
- Grill the patties on the preheated grill or in the pan. For medium burgers, cook for about 4-5 minutes per side. Adjust the time based on your preferred doneness.
- If adding cheese, place a slice on each patty about a minute before they are done cooking to allow it to melt.

Toast the Buns:
- In the last minute of cooking, place the hamburger buns on the grill or in a toaster to lightly toast them.

Assemble the Burgers:

- Once the patties are cooked to your liking, remove them from the grill or pan.
- Assemble the burgers by placing each patty on a toasted bun.

Add Toppings:
- Add your preferred toppings such as lettuce, tomato slices, onion slices, pickles, ketchup, mustard, and mayonnaise.

Serve:
- Serve the classic beef burgers immediately, and enjoy!

Feel free to customize your burgers with additional toppings like bacon, sautéed mushrooms, or avocado slices. These classic beef burgers are a versatile and timeless favorite that you can easily make at home for a delicious and satisfying meal.

Beef and Broccoli

Ingredients:

For the Beef Marinade:

- 1 pound flank steak, thinly sliced against the grain
- 2 tablespoons soy sauce
- 1 tablespoon oyster sauce
- 1 tablespoon cornstarch
- 1 tablespoon vegetable oil

For the Stir-Fry:

- 2 tablespoons vegetable oil, divided
- 3 cups broccoli florets
- 2 cloves garlic, minced
- 1 teaspoon fresh ginger, grated
- 1/2 cup low-sodium beef broth
- 1/4 cup soy sauce
- 2 tablespoons oyster sauce
- 1 tablespoon hoisin sauce
- 2 teaspoons cornstarch mixed with 2 tablespoons water (cornstarch slurry)

For Serving:

- Cooked white or brown rice

Instructions:

Marinate the Beef:
- In a bowl, combine the thinly sliced flank steak with soy sauce, oyster sauce, cornstarch, and vegetable oil. Let it marinate for at least 15-20 minutes.

Prepare the Sauce:
- In a separate bowl, mix together beef broth, soy sauce, oyster sauce, and hoisin sauce.

Cook the Broccoli:
- Heat 1 tablespoon of vegetable oil in a large pan or wok over medium-high heat.

- Add the broccoli florets and stir-fry for 3-4 minutes or until they are crisp-tender. Remove the broccoli from the pan and set it aside.

Cook the Beef:
- Add the remaining tablespoon of oil to the pan.
- Add the marinated beef slices and stir-fry for 2-3 minutes until browned.

Add Aromatics:
- Push the beef to the sides of the pan. Add minced garlic and grated ginger to the center of the pan. Stir-fry for about 30 seconds until fragrant.

Combine and Simmer:
- Add the cooked broccoli back to the pan with the beef.
- Pour in the sauce mixture and stir to coat the beef and broccoli.
- Bring the mixture to a simmer.

Thicken the Sauce:
- Pour the cornstarch slurry into the pan and stir well. Cook for an additional 1-2 minutes or until the sauce thickens.

Serve:
- Serve the Beef and Broccoli over cooked rice.

This homemade Beef and Broccoli is a delicious and satisfying meal that you can enjoy with minimal effort. Adjust the sauce ingredients to your taste and serve it with rice for a complete and tasty dish.

Beef Chili

Ingredients:

- 1.5 pounds ground beef
- 1 large onion, diced
- 3 cloves garlic, minced
- 1 bell pepper, diced (any color)
- 1 jalapeño, seeded and finely chopped (optional for heat)
- 2 cans (14 ounces each) diced tomatoes
- 1 can (15 ounces) kidney beans, drained and rinsed
- 1 can (15 ounces) black beans, drained and rinsed
- 2 tablespoons tomato paste
- 1 cup beef broth
- 2 tablespoons chili powder
- 1 teaspoon ground cumin
- 1 teaspoon smoked paprika
- 1/2 teaspoon dried oregano
- Salt and black pepper to taste
- Olive oil for cooking
- Optional toppings: shredded cheese, sour cream, chopped green onions, cilantro

Instructions:

Sauté Aromatics:
- In a large pot or Dutch oven, heat a drizzle of olive oil over medium heat.
- Add diced onions and cook until softened, about 3-4 minutes.
- Add minced garlic and cook for an additional 1 minute.

Brown Ground Beef:
- Add ground beef to the pot, breaking it up with a spoon. Cook until browned and cooked through.

Add Vegetables:
- Stir in diced bell pepper and jalapeño, and cook for 2-3 minutes until they start to soften.

Seasonings:
- Add chili powder, ground cumin, smoked paprika, dried oregano, salt, and black pepper. Stir well to coat the meat and vegetables.

Tomatoes and Beans:

- Add diced tomatoes, kidney beans, black beans, tomato paste, and beef broth. Stir to combine.

Simmer:
- Bring the chili to a simmer. Reduce the heat to low, cover the pot, and let it simmer for at least 30 minutes to allow the flavors to meld. You can simmer longer for a deeper flavor.

Adjust Seasoning:
- Taste and adjust the seasoning as needed. Add more salt, pepper, or chili powder according to your preferences.

Serve:
- Ladle the beef chili into bowls and serve hot.

Garnish:
- Top with your favorite garnishes like shredded cheese, sour cream, chopped green onions, or cilantro.

This beef chili is a versatile dish that you can customize to your liking. It's perfect for serving a crowd, and any leftovers can be frozen for future meals. Enjoy the rich and comforting flavors of this classic beef chili!

Spaghetti Bolognese

Ingredients:

- 1 pound (450g) ground beef (or a mix of beef and pork)
- 1 tablespoon olive oil
- 1 onion, finely chopped
- 2 carrots, finely diced
- 2 celery stalks, finely diced
- 3 cloves garlic, minced
- 1/2 cup red wine (optional)
- 1 can (14 ounces) crushed tomatoes
- 2 tablespoons tomato paste
- 1 cup beef broth
- 1 teaspoon dried oregano
- 1 teaspoon dried basil
- 1/2 teaspoon dried thyme
- Salt and black pepper to taste
- Pinch of red pepper flakes (optional, for heat)
- 1/2 cup whole milk or heavy cream
- 1 pound (450g) spaghetti
- Grated Parmesan cheese for serving

Instructions:

Cook the Meat:
- Heat olive oil in a large pot or Dutch oven over medium heat. Add the ground beef and cook until browned, breaking it up with a spoon as it cooks.

Sauté Vegetables:
- Add chopped onion, diced carrots, diced celery, and minced garlic to the pot. Cook until the vegetables are softened.

Deglaze with Wine (Optional):
- Pour in the red wine (if using) to deglaze the pot, scraping up any browned bits from the bottom.

Add Tomatoes and Broth:
- Stir in crushed tomatoes, tomato paste, beef broth, dried oregano, dried basil, dried thyme, salt, black pepper, and red pepper flakes (if using). Mix well.

Simmer:
- Bring the sauce to a simmer, then reduce the heat to low. Cover the pot and let it simmer for at least 30 minutes to 1 hour, allowing the flavors to meld and the sauce to thicken. Stir occasionally.

Add Milk or Cream:
- Pour in the whole milk or heavy cream and stir it into the sauce. Simmer for an additional 10-15 minutes.

Cook Spaghetti:
- Meanwhile, cook the spaghetti according to the package instructions in a separate pot of salted boiling water until al dente.

Serve:
- Drain the spaghetti and serve it topped with the Bolognese sauce. Garnish with grated Parmesan cheese.

This Spaghetti Bolognese is a comforting and flavorful meal that is sure to be a hit. The slow-cooked meat sauce develops a deep richness, and the combination of vegetables, tomatoes, and herbs adds layers of delicious flavor. Enjoy your homemade Spaghetti Bolognese with a sprinkle of Parmesan cheese for an authentic touch!

Beef Kabobs with Chimichurri Sauce

Ingredients:

For the Beef Kabobs:

- 1.5 pounds sirloin or ribeye steak, cut into 1-inch cubes
- 1 red bell pepper, cut into chunks
- 1 yellow bell pepper, cut into chunks
- 1 red onion, cut into chunks
- Cherry tomatoes
- Wooden skewers, soaked in water for 30 minutes

For the Marinade:

- 1/4 cup olive oil
- 3 tablespoons soy sauce
- 2 tablespoons red wine vinegar
- 2 cloves garlic, minced
- 1 teaspoon dried oregano
- 1 teaspoon ground cumin
- 1/2 teaspoon smoked paprika
- Salt and black pepper to taste

For the Chimichurri Sauce:

- 1 cup fresh parsley, finely chopped
- 1/4 cup fresh cilantro, finely chopped
- 3 cloves garlic, minced
- 1/2 cup extra-virgin olive oil
- 3 tablespoons red wine vinegar
- 1 teaspoon dried oregano
- 1/2 teaspoon red pepper flakes (adjust to taste)
- Salt and black pepper to taste

Instructions:

Marinate the Beef:
- In a bowl, whisk together all the marinade ingredients.
- Place the cubed steak in a zip-top bag or shallow dish and pour the marinade over it. Marinate in the refrigerator for at least 30 minutes, or ideally, 2-4 hours.

Prepare the Chimichurri Sauce:
- In a bowl, combine all the chimichurri sauce ingredients. Stir well and set aside to let the flavors meld.

Assemble the Kabobs:
- Preheat the grill or grill pan to medium-high heat.
- Thread the marinated beef cubes, bell pepper chunks, red onion chunks, and cherry tomatoes onto the soaked wooden skewers.

Grill the Kabobs:
- Grill the kabobs for 8-10 minutes, turning occasionally, or until the beef is cooked to your desired doneness and has a nice char.

Serve with Chimichurri Sauce:
- Remove the beef kabobs from the grill and let them rest for a few minutes.
- Serve the kabobs with a generous drizzle of chimichurri sauce on top or on the side for dipping.

These beef kabobs with chimichurri sauce are a fantastic combination of smoky, grilled flavors and the bright, herby goodness of the chimichurri. They make for a delicious and visually appealing meal, especially during outdoor gatherings or barbecues. Enjoy!

Beef Enchiladas

Ingredients:

For the Enchilada Filling:

- 1 pound ground beef
- 1 small onion, finely chopped
- 2 cloves garlic, minced
- 1 can (14 ounces) black beans, drained and rinsed
- 1 cup corn kernels (fresh, frozen, or canned)
- 1 teaspoon ground cumin
- 1 teaspoon chili powder
- Salt and black pepper to taste
- 1 cup shredded Mexican blend cheese

For the Enchilada Sauce:

- 2 tablespoons vegetable oil
- 2 tablespoons all-purpose flour
- 2 tablespoons chili powder
- 1 teaspoon ground cumin
- 1/2 teaspoon garlic powder
- 1/4 teaspoon cayenne pepper (optional for heat)
- 1 can (15 ounces) tomato sauce
- 1 cup chicken or beef broth
- Salt to taste

For Assembling and Serving:

- 10-12 small flour or corn tortillas
- 1 cup shredded Mexican blend cheese
- Chopped fresh cilantro for garnish
- Sour cream and sliced jalapeños (optional for serving)

Instructions:

Preheat the Oven:
- Preheat your oven to 350°F (175°C).

Prepare the Enchilada Filling:
- In a skillet over medium heat, cook the ground beef until browned. Drain excess fat.
- Add chopped onions and minced garlic to the skillet and sauté until the onions are translucent.
- Stir in black beans, corn, ground cumin, chili powder, salt, and black pepper. Cook for an additional 2-3 minutes.
- Remove from heat and stir in 1 cup of shredded cheese.

Prepare the Enchilada Sauce:
- In a saucepan, heat vegetable oil over medium heat.
- Stir in flour, chili powder, ground cumin, garlic powder, and cayenne pepper (if using) to create a roux.
- Gradually whisk in tomato sauce and broth. Cook, whisking constantly, until the sauce thickens. Season with salt to taste.

Assemble the Enchiladas:
- Warm the tortillas in a microwave or on a skillet to make them pliable.
- Spoon a portion of the beef filling onto each tortilla and roll it up. Place the enchiladas seam-side down in a baking dish.

Pour the Enchilada Sauce:
- Pour the prepared enchilada sauce over the rolled enchiladas.

Add Cheese and Bake:
- Sprinkle the remaining shredded cheese over the top.
- Bake in the preheated oven for 20-25 minutes or until the cheese is melted and bubbly.

Garnish and Serve:
- Remove from the oven and let it cool slightly.
- Garnish with chopped cilantro and serve with sour cream and sliced jalapeños if desired.

These beef enchiladas are a flavorful and comforting dish. You can customize them by adding your favorite toppings and adjusting the spice level to suit your taste. Enjoy your homemade beef enchiladas!

Beef and Vegetable Stir-Fry

Ingredients:

For the Stir-Fry Sauce:

- 1/4 cup soy sauce
- 2 tablespoons oyster sauce
- 1 tablespoon hoisin sauce
- 1 tablespoon rice vinegar
- 1 tablespoon cornstarch
- 1 tablespoon brown sugar
- 1/2 cup beef broth or water

For the Stir-Fry:

- 1 pound (450g) beef sirloin or flank steak, thinly sliced
- 2 tablespoons vegetable oil, divided
- 3 cups mixed vegetables (broccoli florets, bell peppers, snap peas, carrots, etc.)
- 3 cloves garlic, minced
- 1 tablespoon fresh ginger, grated
- Cooked rice or noodles for serving
- Sesame seeds and sliced green onions for garnish (optional)

Instructions:

Prepare the Stir-Fry Sauce:
- In a bowl, whisk together soy sauce, oyster sauce, hoisin sauce, rice vinegar, cornstarch, brown sugar, and beef broth or water. Set aside.

Slice and Marinate the Beef:
- Thinly slice the beef against the grain. Place the slices in a bowl.
- Pour a few tablespoons of the stir-fry sauce over the beef and let it marinate for about 15-20 minutes.

Stir-Fry the Vegetables:
- Heat 1 tablespoon of vegetable oil in a wok or large skillet over high heat.
- Add the mixed vegetables and stir-fry for 3-4 minutes until they are crisp-tender. Remove the vegetables from the wok and set them aside.

Cook the Beef:
- Add the remaining tablespoon of oil to the wok.

- Add the marinated beef slices and stir-fry for 2-3 minutes until they are browned and cooked through.

Combine and Add Sauce:
- Push the beef to the sides of the wok and add minced garlic and grated ginger to the center. Stir for about 30 seconds until fragrant.
- Add the cooked vegetables back to the wok and pour the stir-fry sauce over the mixture.
- Toss everything together until well coated and heated through.

Serve:
- Serve the beef and vegetable stir-fry over cooked rice or noodles.
- Garnish with sesame seeds and sliced green onions if desired.

This beef and vegetable stir-fry is a versatile dish, and you can easily customize it with your favorite vegetables. The combination of savory beef, crisp vegetables, and flavorful sauce makes for a delicious and nutritious meal. Enjoy!

Beef and Guinness Stew

Ingredients:

- 2 pounds (900g) stewing beef, cut into bite-sized pieces
- Salt and black pepper to taste
- 2-3 tablespoons vegetable oil
- 2 large onions, chopped
- 3 cloves garlic, minced
- 2 tablespoons all-purpose flour
- 2 tablespoons tomato paste
- 2 bottles (24 ounces) Guinness stout or any dark beer
- 2 cups beef broth
- 2 bay leaves
- 1 teaspoon dried thyme
- 4 large carrots, peeled and cut into chunks
- 4 medium potatoes, peeled and cut into chunks
- Fresh parsley for garnish (optional)

Instructions:

Preheat the Oven:
- Preheat your oven to 325°F (163°C).

Season and Brown the Beef:
- Season the stewing beef with salt and black pepper.
- Heat 2 tablespoons of vegetable oil in a large oven-safe pot or Dutch oven over medium-high heat.
- Brown the beef in batches to avoid overcrowding, ensuring a nice sear on each side. Set aside.

Sauté Onions and Garlic:
- In the same pot, add more oil if needed. Sauté the chopped onions until softened, about 5 minutes.
- Add minced garlic and cook for an additional minute.

Add Flour and Tomato Paste:
- Sprinkle the flour over the onions and garlic, stirring constantly for 1-2 minutes to cook off the raw flavor.
- Stir in the tomato paste and cook for another minute.

Deglaze with Guinness:

- Pour in the Guinness stout, scraping the bottom of the pot to release any browned bits.

Add Broth and Seasonings:
- Add beef broth, bay leaves, and dried thyme. Bring the mixture to a simmer.

Return Beef to Pot:
- Return the browned beef to the pot, ensuring it's submerged in the liquid.

Transfer to Oven:
- Cover the pot and transfer it to the preheated oven. Cook for about 2 to 2.5 hours or until the beef is tender.

Add Vegetables:
- About 30 minutes before the end of cooking time, add the carrots and potatoes to the pot. Continue cooking until the vegetables are tender.

Adjust Seasoning and Serve:
- Remove bay leaves, taste the stew, and adjust seasoning if needed.
- Serve the Beef and Guinness Stew hot, garnished with fresh parsley if desired.

This Beef and Guinness Stew is a comforting and robust dish that develops deep flavors during slow cooking. It's perfect served with crusty bread or over mashed potatoes. Enjoy this classic Irish-inspired dish!

Sloppy Joes

Ingredients:

- 1 pound (450g) ground beef
- 1 small onion, finely chopped
- 1/2 green bell pepper, finely chopped
- 2 cloves garlic, minced
- 1/2 cup ketchup
- 1/4 cup tomato sauce
- 2 tablespoons tomato paste
- 2 tablespoons brown sugar
- 1 tablespoon Worcestershire sauce
- 1 tablespoon mustard
- 1/2 teaspoon chili powder (adjust to taste)
- Salt and black pepper to taste
- Hamburger buns for serving

Instructions:

Cook the Ground Beef:
- In a large skillet or pan over medium heat, cook the ground beef, breaking it up with a spoon, until browned and cooked through.

Add Vegetables:
- Add chopped onions and green bell peppers to the skillet. Sauté until the vegetables are softened, about 3-5 minutes.

Add Garlic:
- Add minced garlic to the skillet and cook for an additional 1-2 minutes until fragrant.

Make the Sauce:
- Stir in ketchup, tomato sauce, tomato paste, brown sugar, Worcestershire sauce, mustard, chili powder, salt, and black pepper. Mix well to combine.

Simmer:
- Reduce the heat to low and let the mixture simmer for 10-15 minutes, allowing the flavors to meld and the sauce to thicken.

Adjust Seasoning:
- Taste the Sloppy Joe mixture and adjust the seasoning if needed. Add more salt, pepper, or chili powder to suit your taste.

Serve:

- Spoon the Sloppy Joe mixture onto hamburger buns and serve immediately.

Optional Toppings:
- You can add additional toppings like shredded cheese, sliced pickles, or coleslaw if desired.

Sloppy Joes are versatile and can be customized according to your preferences. They are quick to make and perfect for a casual and satisfying meal. Serve them with your favorite side dishes for a complete and enjoyable experience.

Philly Cheesesteak Sandwich

Ingredients:

For the Steak:

- 1 pound (450g) ribeye or sirloin steak, thinly sliced
- Salt and black pepper to taste
- 1 tablespoon vegetable oil

For the Onions and Peppers:

- 1 large onion, thinly sliced
- 1 bell pepper (green or red), thinly sliced
- 2 tablespoons vegetable oil
- Salt and black pepper to taste

For the Sandwiches:

- 4 hoagie rolls or sub rolls
- 8 slices of provolone or American cheese

Instructions:

Prepare the Steak:
- Thinly slice the steak against the grain. Season the slices with salt and black pepper.

Sauté the Steak:
- Heat vegetable oil in a large skillet or griddle over medium-high heat.
- Add the sliced steak and cook quickly, stirring frequently, until browned and cooked to your liking. This usually takes just a few minutes.

Sauté the Onions and Peppers:
- In the same skillet, add more oil if needed. Add the thinly sliced onions and bell peppers.
- Sauté until the vegetables are soft and slightly caramelized. Season with salt and black pepper to taste.

Assemble the Sandwiches:
- Preheat your oven broiler.
- Split the hoagie rolls and place them on a baking sheet.
- Distribute the sautéed steak evenly over the rolls.

- Top the steak with sautéed onions and peppers.
- Lay slices of provolone or American cheese on top.

Broil the Sandwiches:
- Place the baking sheet under the broiler for 1-2 minutes, or until the cheese is melted and bubbly. Keep a close eye to prevent burning.

Serve:
- Remove the sandwiches from the oven and serve immediately.

Philly Cheesesteak Sandwiches are often served with additional condiments like ketchup or mayonnaise. Feel free to customize the sandwiches to your liking. Enjoy the cheesy, savory goodness of this iconic sandwich!

Korean BBQ Beef

Ingredients:

- 1.5 pounds (680g) thinly sliced beef (ribeye or sirloin)
- 1/2 cup soy sauce
- 1/4 cup brown sugar
- 2 tablespoons sesame oil
- 3 cloves garlic, minced
- 1 tablespoon grated ginger
- 2 tablespoons mirin or rice wine
- 1 tablespoon honey or corn syrup
- 2 green onions, finely chopped
- 1 tablespoon toasted sesame seeds
- Vegetable oil for cooking
- Optional: Sliced green onions and sesame seeds for garnish

Instructions:

Prepare the Marinade:
- In a bowl, whisk together soy sauce, brown sugar, sesame oil, minced garlic, grated ginger, mirin, honey, chopped green onions, and toasted sesame seeds.

Marinate the Beef:
- Place the thinly sliced beef in a large bowl or a resealable plastic bag.
- Pour the marinade over the beef, ensuring that each slice is well-coated.
- Marinate the beef for at least 30 minutes to 2 hours in the refrigerator. For more flavor, you can marinate it overnight.

Cooking Options:
- Grilling: Preheat a grill or grill pan over medium-high heat. Grill the marinated beef slices for 2-3 minutes per side until cooked to your liking.
- Stir-frying: Heat a skillet or wok over medium-high heat. Add a bit of vegetable oil and stir-fry the beef slices until cooked through.

Serve:
- Once cooked, transfer the Korean BBQ beef to a serving plate.
- Garnish with additional sliced green onions and sesame seeds if desired.

Serve with Accompaniments:
- Serve the Korean BBQ beef with steamed rice, lettuce leaves for wrapping (ssam), and any desired side dishes like kimchi or pickled vegetables.

Enjoy the delicious and savory Korean BBQ Beef! You can customize this dish based on your preferences, and it's a great option for a flavorful and satisfying meal.

Beef Satay Skewers

Ingredients:

For the Beef Marinade:

- 1.5 pounds (680g) beef sirloin or flank steak, thinly sliced
- 1/4 cup soy sauce
- 2 tablespoons oyster sauce
- 2 tablespoons brown sugar
- 2 tablespoons vegetable oil
- 1 tablespoon curry powder
- 1 teaspoon ground cumin
- 1 teaspoon turmeric powder
- 2 cloves garlic, minced
- 1 tablespoon grated ginger
- Wooden skewers, soaked in water for 30 minutes

For the Peanut Sauce:

- 1/2 cup creamy peanut butter
- 1/4 cup soy sauce
- 2 tablespoons brown sugar
- 2 tablespoons rice vinegar
- 1 tablespoon sesame oil
- 1 clove garlic, minced
- 1 teaspoon grated ginger
- Water (as needed to adjust consistency)

Instructions:

Prepare the Marinade:
- In a bowl, whisk together soy sauce, oyster sauce, brown sugar, vegetable oil, curry powder, ground cumin, turmeric powder, minced garlic, and grated ginger.
- Add the thinly sliced beef to the marinade, ensuring each slice is well-coated. Marinate for at least 30 minutes to allow the flavors to infuse.

Make the Peanut Sauce:

- In a separate bowl, whisk together peanut butter, soy sauce, brown sugar, rice vinegar, sesame oil, minced garlic, and grated ginger. If the sauce is too thick, thin it with a little water until you reach the desired consistency.

Skewer the Beef:
- Preheat a grill or grill pan to medium-high heat.
- Thread the marinated beef slices onto the soaked wooden skewers.

Grill the Skewers:
- Grill the beef skewers for 2-3 minutes per side or until they are cooked to your liking and have a nice char.

Serve:
- Arrange the Beef Satay Skewers on a serving plate.
- Serve with the prepared Peanut Sauce for dipping.

Garnish (Optional):
- Garnish the skewers with chopped cilantro or sliced green onions if desired.

Enjoy your homemade Beef Satay Skewers with Peanut Sauce! They make for a delicious appetizer or a flavorful main dish, especially when served with steamed rice or as part of a larger Asian-inspired meal.

Pork Recipes:
Pulled Pork Sandwiches

Ingredients:

For the Pulled Pork:

- 3-4 pounds (about 1.5-2 kg) pork shoulder or pork butt
- 2 tablespoons brown sugar
- 1 tablespoon paprika
- 1 tablespoon garlic powder
- 1 tablespoon onion powder
- 1 teaspoon cumin
- 1 teaspoon dried thyme
- 1 teaspoon salt
- 1/2 teaspoon black pepper
- 1 cup chicken broth or apple juice

For the BBQ Sauce:

- 1 cup ketchup
- 1/2 cup apple cider vinegar
- 1/4 cup brown sugar
- 2 tablespoons Dijon mustard
- 1 tablespoon Worcestershire sauce
- 1 teaspoon smoked paprika
- Salt and black pepper to taste

For Serving:

- Hamburger buns or sandwich rolls
- Coleslaw (optional, for topping)

Instructions:

Prepare the Pork:

- In a small bowl, mix together brown sugar, paprika, garlic powder, onion powder, cumin, dried thyme, salt, and black pepper to create a dry rub.
- Rub the dry rub all over the pork shoulder or pork butt, covering it thoroughly. Let it marinate in the refrigerator for at least 1 hour or overnight for better flavor.

Slow Cook the Pork:
- Place the marinated pork in a slow cooker. Pour chicken broth or apple juice around the pork.
- Cook on low for 8-10 hours or until the pork is tender and easily shreds with a fork.

Make the BBQ Sauce:
- In a saucepan over medium heat, combine ketchup, apple cider vinegar, brown sugar, Dijon mustard, Worcestershire sauce, smoked paprika, salt, and black pepper.
- Simmer for 15-20 minutes, stirring occasionally, until the sauce thickens.

Shred the Pork:
- Once the pork is done, remove it from the slow cooker and shred it using two forks. Discard excess fat.

Mix with BBQ Sauce:
- Mix the shredded pork with the prepared BBQ sauce. Adjust the sauce amount to your liking.

Assemble the Sandwiches:
- Toast the hamburger buns or sandwich rolls.
- Spoon a generous amount of pulled pork onto the bottom half of each bun.
- Top with coleslaw if desired, and cover with the other half of the bun.

Serve:
- Serve the Pulled Pork Sandwiches immediately, and enjoy!

Pulled Pork Sandwiches are often served with coleslaw for a refreshing crunch. This dish is perfect for gatherings, barbecues, or a satisfying family meal.

Pork Tenderloin with Apple Cider Glaze

Ingredients:

For the Pork Tenderloin:

- 2 pork tenderloins (about 1 to 1.5 pounds each)
- Salt and black pepper to taste
- 2 tablespoons olive oil

For the Apple Cider Glaze:

- 1 cup apple cider
- 1/4 cup chicken broth
- 2 tablespoons Dijon mustard
- 2 tablespoons maple syrup or honey
- 1 tablespoon soy sauce
- 1 teaspoon cornstarch (optional, for thickening)

For Garnish (optional):

- Fresh thyme or rosemary
- Sliced apples

Instructions:

Preheat the Oven:
- Preheat your oven to 375°F (190°C).

Season the Pork Tenderloin:
- Season the pork tenderloins with salt and black pepper.

Sear the Pork:
- In an oven-safe skillet, heat olive oil over medium-high heat.
- Sear the pork tenderloins on all sides until browned. This should take about 3-4 minutes per side.

Bake the Pork:
- Transfer the skillet to the preheated oven and bake for about 15-20 minutes or until the internal temperature reaches 145°F (63°C) for medium doneness.

Prepare the Apple Cider Glaze:

- In a saucepan, combine apple cider, chicken broth, Dijon mustard, maple syrup or honey, and soy sauce.
- Bring the mixture to a simmer over medium heat. If you prefer a thicker glaze, whisk in cornstarch dissolved in a little water and continue to simmer until thickened.

Glaze the Pork:
- During the last 5-10 minutes of baking, brush the pork tenderloins with the apple cider glaze, coating them evenly. Reserve some glaze for serving.

Rest and Slice:
- Once the pork reaches the desired doneness, remove it from the oven and let it rest for a few minutes before slicing.

Serve:
- Slice the pork tenderloins and drizzle with the remaining apple cider glaze.
- Garnish with fresh thyme or rosemary and sliced apples if desired.

This Pork Tenderloin with Apple Cider Glaze is a perfect balance of sweet and savory flavors. It pairs well with sides like roasted vegetables, mashed potatoes, or a simple green salad. Enjoy this elegant and delicious dish!

Pork Chops with Dijon Mustard Sauce

Ingredients:

For the Pork Chops:

- 4 bone-in pork chops (about 1 inch thick)
- Salt and black pepper to taste
- 2 tablespoons olive oil
- 2 cloves garlic, minced
- 1 teaspoon dried thyme (or 1 tablespoon fresh thyme)

For the Dijon Mustard Sauce:

- 1/2 cup chicken broth
- 1/2 cup heavy cream
- 2 tablespoons Dijon mustard
- 1 tablespoon whole grain mustard
- 1 tablespoon honey or maple syrup
- Salt and black pepper to taste
- Chopped fresh parsley for garnish (optional)

Instructions:

Season and Sear the Pork Chops:
- Season the pork chops generously with salt and black pepper.
- In a large skillet, heat olive oil over medium-high heat. Add the pork chops and sear for about 4-5 minutes on each side or until they are golden brown and have an internal temperature of 145°F (63°C).

Add Garlic and Thyme:
- In the last minute of cooking the pork chops, add minced garlic and dried thyme to the skillet. Sauté for about a minute until fragrant.

Remove Pork Chops:
- Transfer the pork chops to a plate and cover them with foil to keep warm.

Make the Dijon Mustard Sauce:
- In the same skillet, deglaze with chicken broth, scraping up any browned bits from the bottom.

- Add heavy cream, Dijon mustard, whole grain mustard, and honey or maple syrup. Whisk the sauce until it thickens, about 2-3 minutes.

Season and Serve:
- Taste the sauce and adjust the seasoning with salt and black pepper if needed.
- Pour the Dijon Mustard Sauce over the seared pork chops.

Garnish and Serve:
- Garnish with chopped fresh parsley if desired.
- Serve the Pork Chops with Dijon Mustard Sauce immediately.

These pork chops are tender, juicy, and paired with a rich and flavorful Dijon Mustard Sauce. They're perfect when served with mashed potatoes, rice, or your favorite vegetables. Enjoy this delicious and elegant dish!

Cuban Mojo Pork

Ingredients:

For the Marinade (Mojo):

- 1 cup sour orange juice (or 1/2 cup orange juice + 1/2 cup lime juice)
- Zest of 2 oranges
- Zest of 2 limes
- 6 cloves garlic, minced
- 1 teaspoon cumin
- 1 teaspoon dried oregano
- 1 teaspoon salt
- 1/2 teaspoon black pepper
- 1/2 cup olive oil

For the Pork:

- 4-5 pounds pork shoulder (or pork butt), bone-in or boneless

For Roasting:

- 1 cup chicken or vegetable broth
- 1 cup white wine (or additional broth)
- 1 onion, sliced
- 2 oranges, sliced

Instructions:

   Prepare the Marinade (Mojo):
   - In a bowl, combine sour orange juice (or orange and lime juice), orange zest, lime zest, minced garlic, cumin, dried oregano, salt, and black pepper.
   - Whisk in the olive oil to emulsify the marinade.

   Marinate the Pork:
   - Place the pork shoulder in a large resealable plastic bag or a marinating dish.
   - Pour the mojo marinade over the pork, ensuring it's well-coated.
   - Seal the bag or cover the dish and marinate in the refrigerator for at least 4 hours, preferably overnight.

   Preheat the Oven:

- Preheat your oven to 325°F (163°C).

Prepare the Roasting Pan:
- In a roasting pan, add chicken or vegetable broth and white wine (or additional broth).
- Place a rack in the pan to elevate the pork.
- Add sliced onions and oranges to the bottom of the pan.

Roast the Pork:
- Remove the pork from the marinade, allowing excess marinade to drip off.
- Place the pork on the rack in the roasting pan.
- Roast in the preheated oven for approximately 3-4 hours or until the internal temperature reaches at least 190°F (88°C) and the pork is tender.

Baste and Add More Liquid if Needed:
- Occasionally baste the pork with pan juices.
- Add more broth or wine to the pan if it starts to dry out.

Rest and Serve:
- Once done, remove the pork from the oven and let it rest for about 15-20 minutes before slicing.

Slice and Serve:
- Slice the Cuban Mojo Pork and serve with the roasted onions, oranges, and pan juices.

Cuban Mojo Pork is often served with rice, black beans, and plantains. The citrusy marinade infuses the pork with incredible flavor, making it a delicious and authentic Cuban dish. Enjoy!

Pork Carnitas Tacos

Ingredients:

For the Pork Carnitas:

- 3-4 pounds pork shoulder or pork butt, cut into chunks
- 1 onion, roughly chopped
- 4 cloves garlic, minced
- 1 orange, juiced
- 1 lime, juiced
- 1 teaspoon ground cumin
- 1 teaspoon dried oregano
- 1 teaspoon chili powder
- 1 teaspoon smoked paprika
- Salt and black pepper to taste
- 2 tablespoons vegetable oil

For Serving:

- Corn or flour tortillas
- Chopped fresh cilantro
- Diced red onion
- Salsa or pico de gallo
- Lime wedges
- Avocado slices or guacamole

Instructions:

Marinate the Pork:
- In a large bowl, combine pork chunks with chopped onion, minced garlic, orange juice, lime juice, cumin, oregano, chili powder, smoked paprika, salt, and black pepper.
- Allow the pork to marinate for at least 30 minutes, or refrigerate overnight for enhanced flavor.

Slow Cook the Pork:
- Preheat your oven to 325°F (163°C).
- Heat vegetable oil in a large oven-safe pot or Dutch oven over medium-high heat.

- Brown the marinated pork chunks on all sides.
- Once browned, cover the pot and transfer it to the preheated oven.
- Slow cook the pork for about 2.5 to 3 hours, or until the meat is tender and easily shreds with a fork.

Crisp the Carnitas:
- Remove the pot from the oven and shred the pork with two forks.
- Heat a large skillet over medium-high heat.
- Add shredded pork to the skillet in batches, allowing it to crisp up on the edges.

Serve:
- Warm the tortillas.
- Fill the tortillas with the crispy Pork Carnitas.
- Top with chopped cilantro, diced red onion, salsa or pico de gallo, lime wedges, and avocado slices or guacamole.

Enjoy:
- Serve the Pork Carnitas Tacos immediately and enjoy the delicious flavors!

Pork Carnitas Tacos are perfect for a festive meal or a casual dinner with family and friends. Customize the toppings according to your preferences, and savor the rich and savory taste of these tacos.

Honey Mustard Glazed Ham

Ingredients:

- 1 fully cooked ham (bone-in or boneless), about 5-7 pounds
- 1/2 cup Dijon mustard
- 1/4 cup whole grain mustard
- 1/2 cup honey
- 1/4 cup brown sugar
- 2 tablespoons apple cider vinegar
- 1 teaspoon garlic powder
- 1 teaspoon onion powder
- 1/2 teaspoon ground black pepper
- Whole cloves (optional, for garnish)

Instructions:

Preheat the Oven:
- Preheat your oven to 325°F (163°C).

Prepare the Ham:
- If the ham is not pre-sliced, use a sharp knife to score the surface in a diamond pattern, making cuts about 1/2 inch deep. This allows the glaze to penetrate the ham.

Mix the Glaze:
- In a bowl, whisk together Dijon mustard, whole grain mustard, honey, brown sugar, apple cider vinegar, garlic powder, onion powder, and black pepper.

Glaze the Ham:
- Place the ham in a roasting pan.
- Brush a generous amount of the honey mustard glaze over the entire surface of the ham.

Bake:
- Cover the ham with aluminum foil and bake in the preheated oven for about 1.5 to 2 hours, or until the internal temperature reaches 140°F (60°C).

Baste and Caramelize:
- Every 30 minutes, baste the ham with the pan juices and apply more glaze.
- In the last 15-20 minutes of baking, uncover the ham to allow the glaze to caramelize and create a golden brown crust.

Garnish (Optional):
- If desired, insert whole cloves into the ham for decoration.

Rest and Slice:
- Once done, remove the ham from the oven and let it rest for about 15 minutes before slicing.

Serve:
- Slice the Honey Mustard Glazed Ham and serve warm.

This Honey Mustard Glazed Ham is sweet, savory, and has a beautiful golden finish. It pairs well with side dishes like mashed potatoes, roasted vegetables, or a fresh green salad. Enjoy this delicious ham for a festive meal!

Pork and Pineapple Skewers

Ingredients:

- 1.5 pounds pork tenderloin, cut into bite-sized cubes
- 1 cup pineapple chunks (fresh or canned)
- 1/4 cup soy sauce
- 2 tablespoons honey
- 2 tablespoons olive oil
- 2 cloves garlic, minced
- 1 teaspoon ground ginger
- 1 teaspoon smoked paprika
- Salt and black pepper to taste
- Wooden skewers, soaked in water for at least 30 minutes

Instructions:

Prepare the Marinade:
- In a bowl, whisk together soy sauce, honey, olive oil, minced garlic, ground ginger, smoked paprika, salt, and black pepper.

Marinate the Pork:
- Place the pork cubes in a resealable plastic bag or a shallow dish.
- Pour the marinade over the pork, ensuring that all pieces are well-coated.
- Marinate in the refrigerator for at least 30 minutes to allow the flavors to infuse.

Preheat the Grill:
- Preheat your grill or grill pan to medium-high heat.

Assemble the Skewers:
- Thread the marinated pork and pineapple chunks alternately onto the soaked wooden skewers.

Grill the Skewers:
- Place the skewers on the preheated grill and cook for about 10-12 minutes, turning occasionally, until the pork is cooked through and has a nice char.

Baste with Marinade (Optional):
- If desired, you can baste the skewers with some of the remaining marinade during the cooking process.

Serve:

- Once the Pork and Pineapple Skewers are cooked, remove them from the grill and serve immediately.

Garnish (Optional):
- Garnish with chopped cilantro or green onions if desired.

These Pork and Pineapple Skewers are perfect for a summer barbecue or a quick and tasty weeknight dinner. Serve them with rice, couscous, or a side salad for a complete and satisfying meal. Enjoy the delicious combination of savory pork and sweet pineapple!

BBQ Pulled Pork Pizza

Ingredients:

For the Pulled Pork:

- 1.5 pounds pork shoulder or pork butt
- Salt and black pepper to taste
- 1 tablespoon olive oil
- 1 cup barbecue sauce (homemade or store-bought)

For the Pizza:

- Pizza dough (store-bought or homemade)
- Olive oil for brushing
- 1 cup shredded mozzarella cheese
- 1 cup shredded cheddar cheese
- 1 small red onion, thinly sliced
- 1/4 cup chopped fresh cilantro
- 2 tablespoons cornmeal (for dusting the pizza peel)

Instructions:

Prepare the Pulled Pork:

Season the pork shoulder or butt with salt and black pepper.
In a large skillet or Dutch oven, heat olive oil over medium-high heat.
Sear the pork on all sides until browned.
Transfer the pork to a slow cooker and pour barbecue sauce over it.
Cook on low for 6-8 hours or until the pork is tender and easily shreds.

Assemble the Pizza:

Preheat your oven to the highest temperature your oven can reach (usually around 475-500°F or 245-260°C).
Roll out the pizza dough on a lightly floured surface or pizza peel.

If using a pizza stone, sprinkle the pizza peel with cornmeal. If using a baking sheet, lightly grease or use parchment paper.

Transfer the rolled-out dough to the pizza peel or baking sheet.

Brush the surface of the dough with olive oil.

Spread a layer of barbecue sauce over the dough, leaving a small border around the edges.

Sprinkle shredded mozzarella and cheddar cheese evenly over the sauce.

Add pulled pork and sliced red onions on top of the cheese.

Transfer the pizza to the preheated oven and bake for 12-15 minutes or until the crust is golden and the cheese is melted and bubbly.

Remove the pizza from the oven and sprinkle chopped cilantro over the top.

Allow the pizza to cool for a few minutes before slicing.

Serve and enjoy your BBQ Pulled Pork Pizza!

This pizza is a crowd-pleaser, combining the best elements of barbecue and pizza.

Customize it with your favorite toppings and savor the delicious flavors.

Pork Stir-Fry with Vegetables

Ingredients:

For the Marinade:

- 1 pound (450g) pork tenderloin or pork loin, thinly sliced
- 2 tablespoons soy sauce
- 1 tablespoon oyster sauce
- 1 tablespoon cornstarch
- 1 teaspoon sesame oil
- 1 teaspoon sugar
- 1/2 teaspoon black pepper

For the Stir-Fry:

- 2 tablespoons vegetable oil (for cooking)
- 2 bell peppers (different colors), thinly sliced
- 1 medium carrot, julienned
- 1 cup broccoli florets
- 1 cup snow peas, ends trimmed
- 3 green onions, sliced (white and green parts separated)
- 3 cloves garlic, minced
- 1 tablespoon ginger, grated

For the Sauce:

- 3 tablespoons soy sauce
- 2 tablespoons oyster sauce
- 1 tablespoon hoisin sauce
- 1 tablespoon rice vinegar
- 1 teaspoon sesame oil
- 1 teaspoon sugar

Instructions:

Marinate the Pork:

- In a bowl, combine the thinly sliced pork with soy sauce, oyster sauce, cornstarch, sesame oil, sugar, and black pepper. Let it marinate for at least 15-20 minutes.

Prepare the Sauce:
- In a small bowl, whisk together soy sauce, oyster sauce, hoisin sauce, rice vinegar, sesame oil, and sugar to create the sauce. Set aside.

Stir-Fry the Vegetables:
- Heat 1 tablespoon of vegetable oil in a wok or large skillet over high heat.
- Add the sliced bell peppers, julienned carrots, broccoli florets, and snow peas. Stir-fry for 2-3 minutes until the vegetables are crisp-tender. Remove the vegetables from the wok and set aside.

Cook the Pork:
- Add another tablespoon of vegetable oil to the wok.
- Add the marinated pork slices, spreading them out to ensure even cooking. Cook for 2-3 minutes until the pork is browned and cooked through.

Combine and Finish:
- Push the pork to the sides of the wok and add the sliced white parts of the green onions, minced garlic, and grated ginger to the center. Stir-fry for about 1 minute until fragrant.
- Combine the cooked vegetables with the pork in the wok.
- Pour the sauce over the stir-fry and toss everything together until well-coated and heated through.

Serve:
- Garnish with the sliced green parts of the green onions.
- Serve the Pork Stir-Fry with Vegetables over rice or noodles.

This Pork Stir-Fry with Vegetables is a versatile and delicious dish that you can easily customize with your favorite vegetables. It's a great way to enjoy a quick and flavorful meal packed with nutrients.

Sausage and Peppers

Ingredients:

- 1 pound (about 4 links) Italian sausage (sweet or hot), sliced into 1-inch pieces
- 2 tablespoons olive oil
- 1 large onion, thinly sliced
- 2 bell peppers, thinly sliced (use a mix of colors for visual appeal)
- 3 cloves garlic, minced
- 1 can (14 ounces) diced tomatoes, undrained
- 1 teaspoon dried oregano
- 1 teaspoon dried basil
- Salt and black pepper to taste
- Fresh parsley, chopped, for garnish (optional)
- Sub rolls or crusty bread for serving

Instructions:

Cook the Sausage:

- In a large skillet or pan, heat olive oil over medium-high heat.
- Add the sliced sausage and cook until browned on all sides. This usually takes about 5-7 minutes.

Add Vegetables:

- Push the sausage to one side of the skillet and add sliced onions and peppers to the other side.
- Cook the vegetables until they are softened and slightly caramelized, stirring occasionally. This usually takes about 5-7 minutes.

Combine Ingredients:

- Mix the sausage with the cooked onions and peppers in the skillet.
- Add minced garlic and cook for an additional 1-2 minutes until fragrant.

Add Tomatoes and Seasoning:

- Pour in the diced tomatoes with their juices.
- Season with dried oregano, dried basil, salt, and black pepper. Stir to combine.

Simmer:

- Reduce the heat to low and let the mixture simmer for about 15-20 minutes, allowing the flavors to meld.

Garnish and Serve:

- Garnish with fresh parsley if desired.
- Serve the Sausage and Peppers over sub rolls or crusty bread.

This Sausage and Peppers dish is perfect on its own or served in a sandwich. It's a comforting and satisfying meal that's great for family dinners or gatherings. Enjoy the rich and savory flavors of this classic combination!

Pork and Bean Casserole

Ingredients:

- 1.5 pounds pork shoulder or pork butt, cut into bite-sized cubes
- 1 onion, finely chopped
- 2 cloves garlic, minced
- 1 can (15 ounces) navy beans, drained and rinsed
- 1 can (15 ounces) kidney beans, drained and rinsed
- 1 can (15 ounces) black beans, drained and rinsed
- 1 can (14.5 ounces) diced tomatoes, undrained
- 1/2 cup barbecue sauce
- 2 tablespoons tomato paste
- 1 tablespoon Dijon mustard
- 1 tablespoon Worcestershire sauce
- 1 teaspoon smoked paprika
- 1 teaspoon dried thyme
- Salt and black pepper to taste
- 1 cup shredded cheddar cheese (optional, for topping)

Instructions:

Preheat the Oven:
- Preheat your oven to 350°F (175°C).

Sear the Pork:
- In a large oven-safe pot or Dutch oven, heat some oil over medium-high heat.
- Add the pork cubes and brown them on all sides.

Add Aromatics:
- Add the chopped onion and minced garlic to the pot. Sauté until the onions are translucent.

Combine Ingredients:
- Add the drained and rinsed navy beans, kidney beans, and black beans to the pot.
- Pour in the diced tomatoes (with their juice), barbecue sauce, tomato paste, Dijon mustard, Worcestershire sauce, smoked paprika, dried thyme, salt, and black pepper. Stir to combine.

Simmer:

- Bring the mixture to a simmer. Allow it to simmer for about 10-15 minutes to let the flavors meld.

Transfer to the Oven:
- If your pot is oven-safe, you can cover it and transfer it to the preheated oven. If not, transfer the mixture to a large casserole dish.

Bake:
- Bake in the oven for 45 minutes to 1 hour, or until the pork is tender and the flavors have developed.

Optional Cheese Topping:
- If desired, sprinkle shredded cheddar cheese over the top during the last 10 minutes of baking. Allow it to melt and become bubbly.

Serve:
- Once done, remove from the oven and let it rest for a few minutes before serving.

Garnish and Enjoy:
- Garnish with fresh herbs like chopped parsley or cilantro if desired.
- Serve the Pork and Bean Casserole warm.

This Pork and Bean Casserole is a comforting and filling dish that can be served on its own or with a side of crusty bread. It's perfect for a cozy family dinner or a potluck gathering.

Maple Glazed Pork Belly

Ingredients:

- 2 pounds pork belly, skin removed, cut into bite-sized cubes
- 1/2 cup maple syrup
- 1/4 cup soy sauce
- 2 tablespoons rice vinegar
- 1 tablespoon Dijon mustard
- 2 cloves garlic, minced
- 1 teaspoon grated fresh ginger
- 1/2 teaspoon black pepper
- 2 tablespoons vegetable oil
- Green onions, chopped, for garnish (optional)
- Sesame seeds, for garnish (optional)

Instructions:

Marinate the Pork Belly:
- In a bowl, whisk together maple syrup, soy sauce, rice vinegar, Dijon mustard, minced garlic, grated ginger, and black pepper.
- Place the pork belly cubes in a resealable plastic bag or a shallow dish. Pour half of the marinade over the pork, reserving the other half for later. Seal the bag or cover the dish and let it marinate in the refrigerator for at least 1-2 hours, or overnight for better flavor.

Preheat the Oven:
- Preheat your oven to 375°F (190°C).

Sear the Pork Belly:
- Heat vegetable oil in an oven-safe skillet over medium-high heat.
- Remove the pork belly from the marinade and sear the cubes on all sides until browned.

Bake in the Oven:
- Pour the remaining marinade over the seared pork belly.
- Transfer the skillet to the preheated oven and bake for about 45-55 minutes, or until the pork belly is cooked through and has a nice caramelized glaze.

Baste (Optional):
- Baste the pork belly with the pan juices every 15-20 minutes during baking to ensure an even glaze.

Garnish and Serve:
- Once done, remove from the oven.
- Garnish with chopped green onions and sesame seeds if desired.

Rest and Slice:
- Let the Maple Glazed Pork Belly rest for a few minutes before slicing.

Serve Warm:
- Serve the Maple Glazed Pork Belly warm as a delightful appetizer or part of a main course.

This Maple Glazed Pork Belly is a perfect balance of sweet and savory flavors, making it a delectable and indulgent dish. Enjoy the rich and succulent taste of this maple-infused pork belly!

Lamb Recipes:

Grilled Lamb Chops with Mint Pesto

Ingredients:

For the Lamb Chops:

- 8 lamb chops
- Salt and black pepper to taste
- 2 tablespoons olive oil
- 3 cloves garlic, minced
- 1 tablespoon fresh rosemary, chopped

For the Mint Pesto:

- 2 cups fresh mint leaves, packed
- 1/2 cup fresh parsley leaves, packed
- 1/2 cup grated Parmesan cheese
- 1/3 cup toasted pine nuts
- 2 cloves garlic, minced
- 1/2 cup extra-virgin olive oil
- Salt and black pepper to taste
- Juice of 1 lemon

Instructions:

For the Lamb Chops:

> Preheat Grill:
> - Preheat your grill to medium-high heat.
>
> Season Lamb Chops:
> - Season lamb chops with salt, black pepper, minced garlic, and chopped rosemary. Drizzle with olive oil and rub the seasoning onto the lamb.
>
> Grill Lamb Chops:
> - Grill lamb chops for about 4-5 minutes per side for medium-rare, or adjust according to your desired doneness.

For the Mint Pesto:

Prepare Mint Pesto:
- In a food processor, combine mint leaves, parsley, Parmesan cheese, toasted pine nuts, and minced garlic. Pulse until finely chopped.

Stream in Olive Oil:
- With the food processor running, stream in the extra-virgin olive oil until the pesto reaches a smooth consistency.

Season and Add Lemon Juice:
- Season the pesto with salt and black pepper to taste. Add the juice of one lemon and pulse again to combine.

Serve:
- Serve grilled lamb chops drizzled with the mint pesto sauce.

Garnish (Optional):
- Garnish with additional fresh mint leaves or a sprinkle of Parmesan cheese if desired.

This Grilled Lamb Chops with Mint Pesto is a delightful combination of tender grilled lamb and the freshness of mint pesto. It's a perfect dish for special occasions or a gourmet meal at home. Enjoy the vibrant flavors!

Lamb Gyros

Ingredients:

For the Marinade:

- 1.5 pounds boneless lamb leg or shoulder, thinly sliced
- 3 cloves garlic, minced
- 1 teaspoon dried oregano
- 1 teaspoon ground cumin
- 1 teaspoon ground coriander
- 1 teaspoon paprika
- Salt and black pepper to taste
- Juice of 1 lemon
- 3 tablespoons olive oil
- Greek yogurt (optional, for extra tenderness)

For the Tzatziki Sauce:

- 1 cup Greek yogurt
- 1 cucumber, finely diced
- 2 cloves garlic, minced
- 1 tablespoon fresh dill, chopped
- 1 tablespoon fresh mint, chopped (optional)
- 1 tablespoon lemon juice
- Salt and black pepper to taste

For Serving:

- Pita bread or flatbreads
- Sliced tomatoes
- Sliced cucumbers
- Sliced red onions
- Fresh lettuce or shredded cabbage
- Feta cheese (optional)

Instructions:

Marinate the Lamb:

- In a bowl, combine sliced lamb with minced garlic, dried oregano, ground cumin, ground coriander, paprika, salt, black pepper, lemon juice, and olive oil. If you have time, marinate in the refrigerator for at least 1-2 hours, or overnight for more flavor. You can also add Greek yogurt to the marinade for extra tenderness.

Prepare Tzatziki Sauce:
- In a separate bowl, mix Greek yogurt, diced cucumber, minced garlic, chopped dill, mint (if using), lemon juice, salt, and black pepper. Stir well and refrigerate until ready to use.

Cook the Lamb:
- Heat a grill pan or skillet over medium-high heat. Cook the marinated lamb slices for 2-3 minutes per side or until browned and cooked through.

Warm the Flatbreads:
- Warm the pita bread or flatbreads in the oven or on the grill for a minute or two.

Assemble the Gyros:
- Place a few slices of cooked lamb on each flatbread.
- Add sliced tomatoes, cucumbers, red onions, and lettuce or shredded cabbage.

Drizzle with Tzatziki Sauce:
- Drizzle a generous amount of tzatziki sauce over the top.

Optional:
- Optionally, crumble feta cheese on top for added flavor.

Wrap and Serve:
- Roll the flatbread around the fillings, creating a gyro wrap. Secure with foil or parchment paper if needed.

Serve Warm:
- Serve the Lamb Gyros warm, and enjoy!

This homemade Lamb Gyros recipe brings the authentic flavors of Greek street food to your home. Customize the toppings and enjoy this delicious and satisfying dish.

Moroccan Lamb Tagine

Ingredients:

- 2 pounds lamb shoulder or leg, cut into cubes
- 2 tablespoons olive oil
- 1 large onion, finely chopped
- 3 cloves garlic, minced
- 2 teaspoons ground cumin
- 2 teaspoons ground coriander
- 1 teaspoon ground cinnamon
- 1 teaspoon ground ginger
- 1 teaspoon paprika
- 1/2 teaspoon turmeric
- 1/2 teaspoon cayenne pepper (adjust to taste)
- Salt and black pepper to taste
- 1 can (14 ounces) diced tomatoes, undrained
- 1 cup chicken or lamb broth
- 1 cup dried apricots, halved
- 1/2 cup green olives, pitted
- 1/4 cup chopped fresh cilantro or parsley
- Lemon wedges, for serving
- Cooked couscous or rice, for serving

Instructions:

Prepare the Lamb:
- Season lamb cubes with salt and black pepper.

Sear the Lamb:
- In a large tagine, Dutch oven, or deep skillet, heat olive oil over medium-high heat. Brown the lamb cubes on all sides.

Sauté Aromatics:
- Add chopped onions to the tagine and sauté until softened. Add minced garlic and sauté for an additional minute.

Spice Blend:
- Sprinkle ground cumin, ground coriander, ground cinnamon, ground ginger, paprika, turmeric, and cayenne pepper over the lamb and onions. Stir to coat the meat evenly with the spices.

Add Tomatoes and Broth:

- Pour in the diced tomatoes with their juice. Add chicken or lamb broth to the tagine.

Simmer:
- Bring the mixture to a simmer, then reduce the heat to low. Cover and let it simmer for about 1.5 to 2 hours, or until the lamb is tender and the flavors have melded.

Add Apricots and Olives:
- About 30 minutes before the end of cooking, add halved dried apricots and pitted green olives to the tagine. Stir gently.

Check Seasoning:
- Taste and adjust the seasoning if needed, adding more salt, pepper, or spices according to your preference.

Garnish:
- Sprinkle chopped cilantro or parsley over the tagine.

Serve:
- Serve the Moroccan Lamb Tagine over cooked couscous or rice.

Garnish and Enjoy:
- Garnish with lemon wedges and enjoy the flavorful Moroccan Lamb Tagine!

This dish is rich in spices and has a delightful combination of savory and sweet flavors. It's perfect for a comforting and exotic meal at home.

Lamb Kofta

Ingredients:

For the Lamb Kofta:

- 1.5 pounds ground lamb
- 1 small onion, finely grated or minced
- 3 cloves garlic, minced
- 1/4 cup fresh parsley, finely chopped
- 1/4 cup fresh mint, finely chopped
- 1 teaspoon ground cumin
- 1 teaspoon ground coriander
- 1/2 teaspoon ground cinnamon
- 1/2 teaspoon smoked paprika
- 1/4 teaspoon cayenne pepper (adjust to taste)
- Salt and black pepper to taste
- Olive oil (for brushing)

For Serving:

- Pita bread or flatbreads
- Tzatziki sauce or yogurt sauce
- Sliced tomatoes
- Sliced cucumbers
- Red onion, thinly sliced
- Fresh herbs (parsley, mint) for garnish
- Lemon wedges

Instructions:

Prepare the Lamb Mixture:
- In a large bowl, combine ground lamb, grated or minced onion, minced garlic, chopped parsley, chopped mint, ground cumin, ground coriander, ground cinnamon, smoked paprika, cayenne pepper, salt, and black pepper.

Mix Thoroughly:
- Mix the ingredients thoroughly until well combined. You can use your hands for this step.

Shape the Kofta:

- Wet your hands to prevent sticking, then shape the lamb mixture into elongated sausage-like patties or form them onto skewers.

Grill or Bake:
- Grill the lamb kofta on a preheated grill or bake in the oven at 375°F (190°C) for about 15-20 minutes, turning halfway through, or until fully cooked. If using skewers, rotate them for even cooking.

Brush with Olive Oil:
- Brush the kofta with olive oil during grilling or baking to enhance flavor and prevent drying.

Prepare Accompaniments:
- While the kofta is cooking, prepare your accompaniments. Warm the pita bread or flatbreads and gather the sliced tomatoes, cucumbers, red onion, and any desired herbs.

Serve:
- Serve the lamb kofta on the warm pita or flatbreads, topped with sliced tomatoes, cucumbers, and red onion.

Drizzle with Sauce:
- Drizzle with tzatziki sauce or your favorite yogurt-based sauce.

Garnish and Squeeze Lemon:
- Garnish with fresh herbs and squeeze lemon over the top.

Enjoy:
- Enjoy your delicious Lamb Kofta!

This Lamb Kofta recipe provides a burst of Middle Eastern flavors, and the combination of the seasoned lamb with fresh vegetables and sauce makes for a satisfying and tasty meal.

Shepherd's Pie with Lamb

Ingredients:

For the Lamb Filling:

- 1.5 pounds ground lamb
- 1 large onion, finely chopped
- 2 carrots, diced
- 2 cloves garlic, minced
- 1 cup frozen peas
- 2 tablespoons tomato paste
- 1 cup beef or lamb broth
- 1 teaspoon Worcestershire sauce
- 1 teaspoon dried thyme
- 1 teaspoon dried rosemary
- Salt and black pepper to taste
- 2 tablespoons all-purpose flour (optional, for thickening)

For the Mashed Potatoes:

- 2 pounds russet potatoes, peeled and cut into chunks
- 1/2 cup unsalted butter
- 1/2 cup milk (or more for desired consistency)
- Salt and black pepper to taste

Instructions:

For the Lamb Filling:

Brown the Lamb:
- In a large skillet or pan, brown the ground lamb over medium-high heat. Drain any excess fat.

Add Vegetables:
- Add chopped onions, diced carrots, and minced garlic to the skillet. Sauté until the vegetables are softened.

Season and Thicken:
- Season the lamb mixture with salt, black pepper, thyme, and rosemary. Stir in tomato paste.

- If you prefer a thicker filling, you can sprinkle 2 tablespoons of flour over the lamb mixture and stir to combine.

Add Broth and Peas:
- Pour in the beef or lamb broth and Worcestershire sauce. Add frozen peas. Simmer the mixture for about 10 minutes, allowing it to thicken slightly.

Adjust Seasoning:
- Taste and adjust the seasoning if needed. Remove from heat.

For the Mashed Potatoes:

Cook Potatoes:
- Boil or steam the peeled and chopped potatoes until tender.

Mash Potatoes:
- Mash the potatoes with butter and milk until smooth. Season with salt and black pepper to taste.

Assembling and Baking:

Preheat Oven:
- Preheat your oven to 400°F (200°C).

Layer the Shepherd's Pie:
- Spread the lamb filling evenly in a baking dish. Top it with the mashed potatoes, spreading them to cover the lamb.

Create Texture on Potatoes (Optional):
- You can use a fork to create a textured surface on the mashed potatoes, which will brown nicely in the oven.

Bake:
- Bake in the preheated oven for about 20-25 minutes or until the top is golden brown.

Serve:
- Allow the Shepherd's Pie to cool slightly before serving. Serve portions and enjoy!

Shepherd's Pie with lamb is a classic and satisfying meal that's perfect for a cozy dinner. The combination of flavorful lamb filling and creamy mashed potatoes makes it a comfort food favorite.

Rack of Lamb with Rosemary and Garlic

Ingredients:

- 2 racks of lamb, frenched (about 8 ribs each)
- 4 cloves garlic, minced
- 2 tablespoons fresh rosemary, finely chopped
- 2 tablespoons Dijon mustard
- 2 tablespoons olive oil
- Salt and black pepper to taste
- 1 tablespoon balsamic vinegar (optional, for finishing)

Instructions:

Preheat the Oven:
- Preheat your oven to 400°F (200°C).

Prepare the Lamb:
- Pat the racks of lamb dry with paper towels. Season with salt and black pepper.

Make the Marinade:
- In a small bowl, mix together minced garlic, chopped rosemary, Dijon mustard, and olive oil to create the marinade.

Coat the Lamb:
- Brush the lamb racks with the rosemary and garlic marinade, ensuring they are evenly coated on all sides.

Sear the Lamb:
- Heat an oven-safe skillet or pan over medium-high heat. Sear the racks of lamb on all sides until browned. This helps lock in the juices.

Transfer to Oven:
- If your skillet is oven-safe, transfer it to the preheated oven. If not, transfer the seared lamb to a roasting pan.

Roast in the Oven:
- Roast the lamb in the preheated oven for about 15-20 minutes for medium-rare, or adjust the time according to your desired doneness. Use a meat thermometer for accuracy (130°F or 54°C for medium-rare).

Rest the Lamb:
- Once done, remove the lamb from the oven and let it rest for 10 minutes. This allows the juices to redistribute, resulting in a more tender and flavorful meat.

Optional Balsamic Glaze:

- If desired, drizzle the racks of lamb with a bit of balsamic vinegar before serving. This adds a tangy sweetness to complement the richness of the lamb.

Slice and Serve:
- Slice the racks into individual chops and serve on a platter. Garnish with additional fresh rosemary if desired.

Enjoy:
- Enjoy your elegant Rack of Lamb with Rosemary and Garlic!

This dish is not only visually stunning but also boasts a delightful combination of flavors from the rosemary and garlic. It pairs well with side dishes like roasted vegetables or mashed potatoes for a complete and impressive meal.

Lamb and Lentil Soup

Ingredients:

- 1 pound boneless lamb stew meat, cut into bite-sized pieces
- 1 cup dried green or brown lentils, rinsed and drained
- 1 large onion, chopped
- 2 carrots, diced
- 2 celery stalks, diced
- 3 cloves garlic, minced
- 1 can (14 ounces) diced tomatoes, undrained
- 6 cups beef or vegetable broth
- 1 teaspoon ground cumin
- 1 teaspoon ground coriander
- 1 teaspoon smoked paprika
- 1/2 teaspoon ground turmeric
- 1/2 teaspoon dried thyme
- Salt and black pepper to taste
- 2 tablespoons olive oil
- Fresh parsley for garnish (optional)
- Lemon wedges for serving (optional)

Instructions:

Sear the Lamb:
- In a large pot or Dutch oven, heat olive oil over medium-high heat. Add the lamb pieces and brown them on all sides. Remove lamb from the pot and set aside.

Sauté Vegetables:
- In the same pot, add chopped onions, carrots, and celery. Sauté until the vegetables are softened.

Add Garlic and Spices:
- Add minced garlic, ground cumin, ground coriander, smoked paprika, ground turmeric, and dried thyme. Stir well to coat the vegetables with the spices.

Add Lentils and Lamb:
- Return the seared lamb to the pot. Add the rinsed lentils and diced tomatoes with their juice. Mix everything together.

Pour in Broth:

- Pour in the beef or vegetable broth. Bring the soup to a boil, then reduce the heat to low.

Simmer:
- Cover the pot and let the soup simmer for about 45-60 minutes, or until the lamb is tender, and the lentils are cooked.

Season:
- Season the soup with salt and black pepper to taste. Adjust the seasoning as needed.

Garnish and Serve:
- Ladle the hot soup into bowls. Garnish with fresh parsley if desired. Serve with lemon wedges on the side for a burst of citrus flavor.

Enjoy:
- Enjoy your comforting Lamb and Lentil Soup!

This soup is not only delicious but also packed with protein and fiber from the lentils and the savory taste of lamb. It's a wholesome and satisfying meal, especially during colder months.

Greek Lamb Souvlaki

Ingredients:

For the Marinade:

- 1.5 pounds lamb leg or shoulder, cut into cubes
- 1/4 cup olive oil
- 3 tablespoons red wine vinegar
- 3 cloves garlic, minced
- 1 teaspoon dried oregano
- 1 teaspoon dried thyme
- 1 teaspoon paprika
- Salt and black pepper to taste

For Serving:

- Pita bread
- Tzatziki sauce
- Sliced tomatoes
- Sliced cucumbers
- Red onion, thinly sliced
- Fresh parsley, chopped
- Lemon wedges

Instructions:

Prepare the Marinade:
- In a bowl, whisk together olive oil, red wine vinegar, minced garlic, dried oregano, dried thyme, paprika, salt, and black pepper to create the marinade.

Marinate the Lamb:
- Place the lamb cubes in a shallow dish or resealable plastic bag. Pour the marinade over the lamb, ensuring it's well-coated. Marinate in the refrigerator for at least 1-2 hours, or overnight for enhanced flavor.

Preheat Grill:
- Preheat your grill or grill pan to medium-high heat.

Skewer the Lamb:

- Thread the marinated lamb cubes onto skewers, leaving space between each piece.

Grill the Souvlaki:
- Grill the lamb skewers for about 8-10 minutes, turning occasionally, until the lamb is cooked to your desired doneness and has a nice char.

Warm Pita Bread:
- In the last few minutes of grilling, warm the pita bread on the grill until it's slightly toasted.

Assemble the Souvlaki:
- Remove the lamb skewers from the grill. Place them on a serving platter.

Serve:
- Serve the Greek Lamb Souvlaki with warmed pita bread. Garnish with sliced tomatoes, cucumbers, red onion, and chopped fresh parsley.

Drizzle with Tzatziki:
- Drizzle tzatziki sauce over the souvlaki or serve it on the side. You can also add a squeeze of lemon juice for extra freshness.

Enjoy:
- Enjoy your homemade Greek Lamb Souvlaki with all the delicious accompaniments!

This dish captures the authentic flavors of Greek cuisine, and the combination of the well-marinated grilled lamb with the freshness of vegetables and tzatziki sauce creates a delightful and satisfying meal.

Lamb Shank Stew

Ingredients:

- 4 lamb shanks
- 2 tablespoons olive oil
- 1 large onion, finely chopped
- 3 carrots, peeled and diced
- 3 celery stalks, diced
- 4 cloves garlic, minced
- 2 tablespoons tomato paste
- 1 cup red wine
- 4 cups beef or lamb broth
- 1 can (14 ounces) diced tomatoes, undrained
- 2 bay leaves
- 1 teaspoon dried thyme
- 1 teaspoon dried rosemary
- Salt and black pepper to taste
- 1/4 cup all-purpose flour (optional, for thickening)
- Fresh parsley, chopped (for garnish)

Instructions:

Preheat Oven:
- Preheat your oven to 325°F (163°C).

Brown the Lamb Shanks:
- In a large oven-safe pot or Dutch oven, heat olive oil over medium-high heat. Brown the lamb shanks on all sides. Remove the shanks and set them aside.

Sauté Vegetables:
- In the same pot, add chopped onions, diced carrots, diced celery, and minced garlic. Sauté until the vegetables are softened.

Add Tomato Paste:
- Stir in the tomato paste and cook for 2 minutes to enhance the flavor.

Deglaze with Wine:
- Pour in the red wine to deglaze the pot, scraping up any browned bits from the bottom.

Add Broth and Tomatoes:

- Return the browned lamb shanks to the pot. Add beef or lamb broth, diced tomatoes with their juice, bay leaves, dried thyme, dried rosemary, salt, and black pepper.

Bring to Simmer:
- Bring the stew to a simmer on the stovetop.

Optional Thickening:
- If you prefer a thicker stew, you can sprinkle 1/4 cup of all-purpose flour over the lamb and vegetables. Stir well to combine.

Cover and Transfer to Oven:
- Cover the pot with a lid and transfer it to the preheated oven. Let it cook for about 2.5 to 3 hours or until the lamb is tender and falling off the bone.

Check and Adjust:
- Occasionally check the stew and adjust the seasoning if needed.

Serve:
- Once the lamb shanks are tender, remove the pot from the oven. Discard the bay leaves.

Garnish and Enjoy:
- Serve the Lamb Shank Stew in bowls, garnished with chopped fresh parsley.

This Lamb Shank Stew is a comforting and flavorful dish, with the slow-cooked lamb delivering a melt-in-your-mouth experience. It's perfect for a cozy dinner, especially during colder months.

Lamb Curry

Ingredients:

- 2 pounds boneless lamb, cut into bite-sized pieces
- 3 tablespoons vegetable oil
- 2 large onions, finely chopped
- 4 cloves garlic, minced
- 1-inch piece of ginger, grated
- 2 tomatoes, chopped
- 1 cup yogurt
- 2 tablespoons tomato paste
- 1 cup water or lamb broth
- Salt to taste

Spice Blend:

- 2 teaspoons ground coriander
- 2 teaspoons ground cumin
- 1 teaspoon turmeric powder
- 1 teaspoon red chili powder (adjust to taste)
- 1 teaspoon garam masala
- 1/2 teaspoon ground cinnamon
- 1/2 teaspoon ground cardamom
- 1/4 teaspoon ground cloves

For Garnish:

- Fresh cilantro, chopped
- Sliced green chilies (optional)
- Lemon wedges

Instructions:

Prepare the Spice Blend:
- In a small bowl, mix together ground coriander, ground cumin, turmeric powder, red chili powder, garam masala, ground cinnamon, ground cardamom, and ground cloves. Set aside.

Brown the Lamb:

- Heat vegetable oil in a large pot over medium-high heat. Brown the lamb pieces in batches, ensuring they are well-seared on all sides. Remove the lamb and set aside.

Sauté Onions, Garlic, and Ginger:
- In the same pot, add chopped onions and sauté until golden brown. Add minced garlic and grated ginger, and cook for an additional 1-2 minutes.

Add Spice Blend:
- Sprinkle the prepared spice blend over the onions, garlic, and ginger. Stir well to coat the mixture with the spices.

Stir in Tomatoes:
- Add chopped tomatoes and tomato paste. Cook until the tomatoes are soft and the oil starts to separate from the mixture.

Reintroduce Browned Lamb:
- Return the browned lamb pieces to the pot. Stir well to coat the lamb with the spice and tomato mixture.

Incorporate Yogurt:
- Whisk the yogurt and gradually add it to the lamb, stirring continuously to prevent curdling.

Add Water or Broth:
- Pour in water or lamb broth to create a curry consistency. Stir, cover the pot, and simmer over low heat for about 1.5 to 2 hours or until the lamb is tender. Stir occasionally and add more water if needed.

Adjust Seasoning:
- Taste and adjust the seasoning by adding salt as needed.

Garnish and Serve:
- Garnish the Lamb Curry with chopped cilantro and sliced green chilies if you like it spicy. Serve with rice or Indian bread (naan or roti) and lemon wedges.

Enjoy:
- Enjoy your flavorful and aromatic Lamb Curry!

This Lamb Curry is rich in spices and has a wonderful depth of flavor. Adjust the spice level according to your preference, and feel free to customize it with additional ingredients like potatoes or peas if desired.

Turkey Recipes:

Thanksgiving Roast Turkey

Ingredients:

- 1 whole turkey (12-15 pounds), thawed if frozen
- 1 cup (2 sticks) unsalted butter, softened
- Salt and black pepper to taste
- 1 tablespoon dried sage
- 1 tablespoon dried thyme
- 1 tablespoon dried rosemary
- 1 tablespoon paprika
- 1 onion, quartered
- 1 lemon, halved
- 4-5 garlic cloves, peeled
- Fresh herbs for garnish (optional)
- Turkey broth or chicken broth for basting

Instructions:

Preheat Oven:
- Preheat your oven to 325°F (163°C).

Prepare the Turkey:
- Remove the turkey from its packaging and pat it dry with paper towels. Make sure to remove the neck and giblets from the cavity.

Season the Turkey:
- In a small bowl, mix together softened butter, dried sage, dried thyme, dried rosemary, paprika, salt, and black pepper to create a seasoned butter mixture.

Apply Seasoned Butter:
- Carefully separate the skin from the turkey breast and rub half of the seasoned butter under the skin. Rub the remaining butter over the outside of the turkey.

Stuff the Cavity:
- Place quartered onion, halved lemon, and peeled garlic cloves inside the turkey cavity. This will add flavor to the bird as it roasts.

Truss the Turkey (Optional):

- Trussing is the process of tying the turkey's legs together with kitchen twine to ensure even cooking. While optional, it can help the turkey cook more evenly.

Place in Roasting Pan:
- Place the turkey on a rack in a roasting pan, breast side up. Tuck the wing tips under the turkey.

Basting:
- Baste the turkey with turkey or chicken broth every 30 minutes to keep it moist.

Roast:
- Roast the turkey in the preheated oven. The general rule is about 15 minutes of cooking time per pound. Use a meat thermometer to ensure the internal temperature reaches at least 165°F (74°C) in the thickest part of the thigh.

Resting:
- Once the turkey is cooked, let it rest for at least 20-30 minutes before carving. This allows the juices to redistribute, resulting in a moist and flavorful turkey.

Carve and Serve:
- Carve the turkey, garnish with fresh herbs if desired, and serve with your favorite Thanksgiving sides.

Enjoy:
- Enjoy your Thanksgiving Roast Turkey with family and friends!

Feel free to customize this recipe by adding your favorite herbs or using a brine for extra flavor. Additionally, you can stuff the turkey with your preferred stuffing if desired. Happy Thanksgiving!

Turkey Meatballs

Ingredients:

For the Meatballs:

- 1 pound ground turkey (preferably a mix of dark and light meat)
- 1/2 cup breadcrumbs
- 1/4 cup grated Parmesan cheese
- 1/4 cup chopped fresh parsley
- 1/4 cup finely chopped onion
- 2 cloves garlic, minced
- 1 large egg
- 1 teaspoon dried oregano
- 1 teaspoon dried basil
- Salt and black pepper to taste
- Olive oil for cooking

For the Sauce (optional):

- 1 can (14 ounces) crushed tomatoes
- 2 cloves garlic, minced
- 1 teaspoon dried oregano
- Salt and black pepper to taste
- Fresh basil, chopped (for garnish)

Instructions:

For the Meatballs:

    Preheat Oven:
- Preheat your oven to 375°F (190°C).

    Mix Ingredients:
- In a large bowl, combine ground turkey, breadcrumbs, Parmesan cheese, chopped parsley, chopped onion, minced garlic, egg, dried oregano, dried basil, salt, and black pepper. Mix until well combined.

    Shape Meatballs:
- Scoop out portions of the mixture and shape them into meatballs, about 1 to 1.5 inches in diameter. Place them on a baking sheet lined with parchment paper.

    Bake:

- Bake in the preheated oven for 20-25 minutes or until the meatballs are cooked through and browned on the outside.

Optional: Sear in a Pan (for extra color):
- If you prefer a golden-brown exterior, you can sear the baked meatballs in a hot pan with a bit of olive oil for a few minutes.

For the Sauce (optional):

Prepare the Sauce:
- In a saucepan, combine crushed tomatoes, minced garlic, dried oregano, salt, and black pepper. Simmer over low heat for about 10-15 minutes.

Serve:
- Once the meatballs are cooked, you can either add them to the sauce or serve them separately.

Garnish:
- Garnish with fresh chopped basil before serving.

Enjoy:
- Enjoy your turkey meatballs on their own, with pasta, or as part of a sub sandwich!

These turkey meatballs are versatile and can be used in various dishes. They're a healthier option, and the addition of herbs and Parmesan gives them a delightful flavor.

Turkey and Cranberry Panini

Ingredients:

- Sliced turkey (leftover Thanksgiving turkey works well)
- Cranberry sauce
- Sliced Swiss or provolone cheese
- Stuffing (optional)
- Sliced bread (ciabatta, sourdough, or your choice)
- Butter or olive oil for grilling

Instructions:

Preheat Panini Press or Grill Pan:
- If you have a Panini press, preheat it. If not, you can use a grill pan on the stove.

Assemble the Panini:
- Take two slices of bread. On one slice, layer sliced turkey, a spoonful of cranberry sauce, sliced cheese, and stuffing if desired. Top with the second slice of bread.

Butter or Oil:
- Lightly butter or brush olive oil on the outer sides of the sandwich. This will help it crisp up and get that golden color when grilled.

Grill the Panini:
- Place the sandwich on the preheated Panini press or grill pan. Grill for 3-5 minutes or until the bread is golden brown, and the cheese is melted.

Flip and Grill Other Side:
- If using a Panini press, close the lid and grill the other side for an additional 3-5 minutes. If using a grill pan, carefully flip the sandwich and grill the other side until it's golden brown and the cheese is melted.

Slice and Serve:
- Remove the Turkey and Cranberry Panini from the press or pan. Allow it to rest for a moment before slicing it in half.

Enjoy:
- Serve your Turkey and Cranberry Panini warm and enjoy the delicious combination of flavors.

This panini is a great way to use up Thanksgiving leftovers, and the combination of turkey, cranberry sauce, and cheese makes it a delightful and comforting sandwich. Feel free to customize it with your favorite bread or additional ingredients!

Ground Turkey Chili

Ingredients:

- 1 pound ground turkey
- 1 tablespoon olive oil
- 1 onion, diced
- 3 cloves garlic, minced
- 1 bell pepper, diced (any color)
- 1 can (14 ounces) diced tomatoes
- 1 can (15 ounces) kidney beans, drained and rinsed
- 1 can (15 ounces) black beans, drained and rinsed
- 1 cup corn kernels (fresh, frozen, or canned)
- 1 can (6 ounces) tomato paste
- 3 cups chicken or vegetable broth
- 2 teaspoons ground cumin
- 2 teaspoons chili powder
- 1 teaspoon dried oregano
- 1 teaspoon smoked paprika
- Salt and black pepper to taste
- Optional toppings: shredded cheese, sour cream, chopped green onions, cilantro

Instructions:

Sauté Ground Turkey:
- In a large pot, heat olive oil over medium heat. Add ground turkey and cook until browned, breaking it apart with a spoon as it cooks.

Add Aromatics:
- Add diced onions and minced garlic to the browned turkey. Sauté for a few minutes until the onions are softened.

Add Bell Pepper:
- Stir in diced bell pepper and cook for an additional 2-3 minutes until the pepper begins to soften.

Add Tomatoes and Tomato Paste:
- Add diced tomatoes and tomato paste to the pot. Stir to combine with the turkey and vegetables.

Add Beans and Corn:
- Add drained and rinsed kidney beans, black beans, and corn kernels to the pot. Mix well.

Season the Chili:

- Sprinkle ground cumin, chili powder, dried oregano, smoked paprika, salt, and black pepper over the mixture. Stir to evenly distribute the spices.

Pour in Broth:
- Pour in the chicken or vegetable broth, ensuring it covers the ingredients. Bring the chili to a simmer.

Simmer:
- Reduce the heat to low, cover the pot, and let the chili simmer for at least 30 minutes to allow the flavors to meld. You can simmer longer for a richer flavor.

Adjust Seasoning:
- Taste and adjust the seasoning if needed. Add more salt, pepper, or spices according to your preference.

Serve:
- Ladle the Ground Turkey Chili into bowls. Top with shredded cheese, sour cream, chopped green onions, or cilantro if desired.

Enjoy:
- Serve the chili hot and enjoy a comforting and flavorful meal!

This Ground Turkey Chili is not only delicious but also versatile. Feel free to customize it by adding your favorite chili toppings or adjusting the spice level to suit your taste.

Turkey and Avocado Wrap

Ingredients:

- 1 large whole wheat or spinach tortilla
- 4-6 slices of deli turkey
- 1/2 avocado, sliced
- 1/2 cup cherry tomatoes, halved
- 1/4 cup cucumber, thinly sliced
- 1/4 cup red onion, thinly sliced
- 1/4 cup shredded lettuce or spinach
- 1 tablespoon mayonnaise or Greek yogurt
- 1 teaspoon Dijon mustard (optional)
- Salt and black pepper to taste

Instructions:

Prepare the Ingredients:
- Slice the avocado, halve the cherry tomatoes, thinly slice the cucumber and red onion, and shred the lettuce or spinach.

Warm the Tortilla:
- If you prefer a warm wrap, you can briefly heat the tortilla in a dry skillet or microwave for about 10 seconds.

Assemble the Wrap:
- Lay the tortilla flat on a clean surface. Spread mayonnaise or Greek yogurt over the center of the tortilla. If desired, add Dijon mustard for extra flavor.

Layer the Ingredients:
- Place the deli turkey slices in the center of the tortilla. Add sliced avocado, halved cherry tomatoes, sliced cucumber, red onion, and shredded lettuce or spinach.

Season and Roll:
- Sprinkle salt and black pepper over the ingredients. Carefully fold in the sides of the tortilla, and then roll it up tightly from the bottom, creating a wrap.

Secure and Cut:
- If needed, secure the wrap with toothpicks, and then cut it in half diagonally for easier handling.

Serve:
- Place the Turkey and Avocado Wrap on a plate and serve immediately.

Enjoy:

- Enjoy your quick and nutritious Turkey and Avocado Wrap!

Feel free to customize the wrap with your favorite ingredients or add a drizzle of balsamic glaze for extra flavor. This versatile recipe allows you to tailor it to your taste preferences while providing a satisfying and healthy meal.

Turkey and Avocado Wrap

Ingredients:

- 1 large whole wheat or spinach tortilla
- 4-6 slices of deli turkey
- 1/2 avocado, sliced
- 1/2 cup cherry tomatoes, halved
- 1/4 cup cucumber, thinly sliced
- 1/4 cup red onion, thinly sliced
- 1/4 cup shredded lettuce or spinach
- 1 tablespoon mayonnaise or Greek yogurt
- 1 teaspoon Dijon mustard (optional)
- Salt and black pepper to taste

Instructions:

Prepare the Ingredients:

- Slice the avocado, halve the cherry tomatoes, thinly slice the cucumber and red onion, and shred the lettuce or spinach.

Warm the Tortilla:

- If you prefer a warm wrap, you can briefly heat the tortilla in a dry skillet or microwave for about 10 seconds.

Assemble the Wrap:

- Lay the tortilla flat on a clean surface. Spread mayonnaise or Greek yogurt over the center of the tortilla. If desired, add Dijon mustard for extra flavor.

Layer the Ingredients:

- Place the deli turkey slices in the center of the tortilla. Add sliced avocado, halved cherry tomatoes, sliced cucumber, red onion, and shredded lettuce or spinach.

Season and Roll:

- Sprinkle salt and black pepper over the ingredients. Carefully fold in the sides of the tortilla, and then roll it up tightly from the bottom, creating a wrap.

Secure and Cut:

- If needed, secure the wrap with toothpicks, and then cut it in half diagonally for easier handling.

Serve:

- Place the Turkey and Avocado Wrap on a plate and serve immediately.

Enjoy:

- Enjoy your quick and nutritious Turkey and Avocado Wrap!

Feel free to customize the wrap with your favorite ingredients or add a drizzle of balsamic glaze for extra flavor. This versatile recipe allows you to tailor it to your taste preferences while providing a satisfying and healthy meal.

Turkey Pot Pie

Ingredients:

For the Filling:

- 2 cups cooked turkey, shredded or diced
- 2 tablespoons butter
- 1 onion, diced
- 2 carrots, diced
- 2 celery stalks, diced
- 1/2 cup frozen peas
- 1/2 cup frozen corn
- 1/4 cup all-purpose flour
- 2 cups turkey or chicken broth
- 1 cup milk
- Salt and black pepper to taste
- 1 teaspoon dried thyme
- 1 teaspoon dried sage

For the Pie Crust:

- 2 store-bought or homemade pie crusts

Instructions:

For the Filling:

    Preheat Oven:
- Preheat your oven to 425°F (218°C).

    Sauté Vegetables:
- In a large skillet, melt the butter over medium heat. Add diced onion, carrots, and celery. Sauté until the vegetables are softened.

    Add Flour:
- Sprinkle the flour over the vegetables and stir to combine. Cook for 1-2 minutes to eliminate the raw flour taste.

    Pour in Broth and Milk:
- Gradually pour in the turkey or chicken broth and milk, stirring continuously to avoid lumps. Bring the mixture to a simmer.

    Season and Add Turkey:

- Add shredded or diced turkey, frozen peas, frozen corn, dried thyme, dried sage, salt, and black pepper. Stir well to combine. Simmer for 5-7 minutes until the mixture thickens.

For the Pie Crust:

Prepare Pie Crust:
- Roll out one pie crust and place it in a pie dish. Press it gently against the bottom and sides.

Fill Pie:
- Pour the turkey and vegetable filling into the pie crust.

Cover with Second Crust:
- Roll out the second pie crust and place it over the filling. Trim and crimp the edges to seal the pie.

Ventilation:
- Cut a few slits in the top crust to allow steam to escape.

Bake:
- Place the pot pie in the preheated oven and bake for 30-35 minutes or until the crust is golden brown.

Cool and Serve:
- Allow the Turkey Pot Pie to cool for a few minutes before slicing. Serve warm and enjoy!

Feel free to customize the filling with other vegetables or herbs you have on hand. This Turkey Pot Pie is a great way to use up leftovers and enjoy a comforting, hearty meal.

Turkey Tetrazzini

Ingredients:

- 8 oz (about 226g) spaghetti or fettuccine noodles
- 2 tablespoons unsalted butter
- 1/2 cup diced onion
- 1/2 cup diced celery
- 1/2 cup sliced mushrooms
- 2 cloves garlic, minced
- 1/4 cup all-purpose flour
- 2 cups turkey or chicken broth
- 1 cup milk
- 1/2 cup heavy cream
- 1 cup shredded Parmesan cheese
- Salt and black pepper to taste
- 2 cups cooked turkey, shredded
- 1/2 cup frozen peas
- 1/4 cup chopped fresh parsley
- 1/2 cup breadcrumbs (optional, for topping)

Instructions:

Preheat Oven:
- Preheat your oven to 375°F (190°C).

Cook Noodles:
- Cook the spaghetti or fettuccine noodles according to the package instructions. Drain and set aside.

Sauté Vegetables:
- In a large skillet, melt the butter over medium heat. Add diced onion, diced celery, sliced mushrooms, and minced garlic. Sauté until the vegetables are softened.

Make Roux:
- Sprinkle the flour over the sautéed vegetables and stir to create a roux. Cook for 1-2 minutes to eliminate the raw flour taste.

Add Broth and Milk:
- Gradually whisk in the turkey or chicken broth, milk, and heavy cream. Continue stirring until the mixture thickens.

Add Cheese:

- Stir in the shredded Parmesan cheese until it's melted and the sauce is smooth. Season with salt and black pepper to taste.

Combine with Turkey and Noodles:
- Add the shredded turkey, cooked noodles, frozen peas, and chopped parsley to the skillet. Mix well to combine all the ingredients evenly.

Transfer to Baking Dish:
- Transfer the mixture to a greased baking dish.

Optional Topping:
- If desired, sprinkle breadcrumbs evenly over the top for a crunchy topping.

Bake:
- Bake in the preheated oven for 25-30 minutes or until the Tetrazzini is bubbly and golden brown on top.

Cool and Serve:
- Allow the Turkey Tetrazzini to cool for a few minutes before serving.

Enjoy:
- Serve warm and enjoy your comforting Turkey Tetrazzini!

This dish is a great way to repurpose leftover turkey into a delicious and creamy casserole. Feel free to customize it with your favorite vegetables or herbs.

Grilled Turkey Burgers

Ingredients:

- 1 pound ground turkey
- 1/4 cup breadcrumbs
- 1/4 cup finely chopped onion
- 1/4 cup finely chopped fresh parsley
- 1 clove garlic, minced
- 1 teaspoon Dijon mustard
- 1 teaspoon Worcestershire sauce
- Salt and black pepper to taste
- Olive oil (for brushing the grill)
- Hamburger buns
- Lettuce, tomatoes, onions, pickles, and condiments for topping

Instructions:

Preheat the Grill:
- Preheat your grill to medium-high heat.

Prepare the Burger Mixture:
- In a large bowl, combine ground turkey, breadcrumbs, chopped onion, chopped parsley, minced garlic, Dijon mustard, Worcestershire sauce, salt, and black pepper. Mix the ingredients until well combined.

Form Burger Patties:
- Divide the mixture into equal portions and shape them into burger patties. Ensure they are not too thick to ensure even cooking.

Oil the Grill:
- Brush the grill grates with a bit of olive oil to prevent sticking.

Grill the Turkey Burgers:
- Place the turkey burgers on the preheated grill. Grill for about 5-6 minutes per side or until the internal temperature reaches 165°F (74°C) and the burgers are cooked through.

Toast the Buns (Optional):
- In the last couple of minutes of grilling, you can place the hamburger buns on the grill to toast them lightly.

Assemble the Burgers:
- Remove the turkey burgers from the grill. Place each burger on a bun and add your favorite toppings such as lettuce, tomatoes, onions, pickles, and condiments.

Serve:
- Serve the grilled turkey burgers immediately.

Enjoy:
- Enjoy your lean and flavorful grilled turkey burgers!

Feel free to customize the burgers with your preferred seasonings or add cheese for an extra layer of flavor. These turkey burgers are a healthy and tasty option for a summer barbecue or any casual meal.

Turkey and Vegetable Skewers

Ingredients:

For the Marinade:

- 1/4 cup olive oil
- 2 tablespoons soy sauce
- 2 tablespoons honey
- 2 cloves garlic, minced
- 1 teaspoon Dijon mustard
- 1 teaspoon dried oregano
- Salt and black pepper to taste

For the Skewers:

- 1.5 pounds turkey breast or turkey tenderloin, cut into cubes
- Cherry tomatoes
- Bell peppers, cut into chunks (assorted colors)
- Red onion, cut into chunks
- Zucchini, sliced
- Mushrooms, whole or halved
- Wooden or metal skewers

Instructions:

Prepare the Marinade:
- In a small bowl, whisk together olive oil, soy sauce, honey, minced garlic, Dijon mustard, dried oregano, salt, and black pepper. This will be the marinade for the turkey and vegetables.

Marinate the Turkey:
- Place the turkey cubes in a large bowl and pour half of the marinade over them. Toss to coat the turkey evenly. Cover and let it marinate in the refrigerator for at least 30 minutes (or longer if time allows).

Prepare Vegetables:
- While the turkey is marinating, prepare the vegetables by cutting them into bite-sized pieces.

Assemble Skewers:
- If using wooden skewers, soak them in water for about 30 minutes to prevent burning. Assemble the skewers by threading marinated turkey cubes and assorted vegetables onto the skewers.

Brush with Marinade:
- Brush the assembled skewers with the remaining marinade for extra flavor.

Preheat Grill:
- Preheat the grill to medium-high heat.

Grill the Skewers:
- Place the turkey and vegetable skewers on the preheated grill. Grill for about 10-15 minutes, turning occasionally, until the turkey is cooked through and the vegetables are tender and slightly charred.

Serve:
- Remove the skewers from the grill and serve immediately.

Enjoy:
- Enjoy the delicious Turkey and Vegetable Skewers with your favorite sides!

These skewers are not only tasty but also a great way to incorporate lean turkey and a variety of colorful vegetables into your meal. Customize the vegetable selection based on your preferences and what's in season.

Turkey Lasagna

Ingredients:

For the Meat Sauce:

- 1 pound ground turkey
- 1 tablespoon olive oil
- 1 onion, finely chopped
- 2 cloves garlic, minced
- 1 bell pepper, diced
- 1 carrot, grated
- 1 can (28 ounces) crushed tomatoes
- 1 can (6 ounces) tomato paste
- 1 teaspoon dried oregano
- 1 teaspoon dried basil
- Salt and black pepper to taste

For the Ricotta Filling:

- 2 cups ricotta cheese
- 1 large egg
- 1/4 cup grated Parmesan cheese
- 1 tablespoon chopped fresh basil
- Salt and black pepper to taste

Other Ingredients:

- 9 lasagna noodles, cooked according to package instructions
- 2 cups shredded mozzarella cheese
- Fresh basil leaves for garnish (optional)

Instructions:

For the Meat Sauce:

Cook Ground Turkey:
- In a large skillet, heat olive oil over medium heat. Add ground turkey and cook until browned, breaking it apart with a spoon.

Sauté Vegetables:
- Add chopped onion, minced garlic, diced bell pepper, and grated carrot to the skillet. Sauté until the vegetables are softened.

Add Tomatoes and Seasonings:
- Stir in crushed tomatoes, tomato paste, dried oregano, dried basil, salt, and black pepper. Simmer the sauce for about 15-20 minutes, allowing the flavors to meld.

For the Ricotta Filling:

Prepare Ricotta Mixture:
- In a bowl, combine ricotta cheese, egg, grated Parmesan cheese, chopped fresh basil, salt, and black pepper. Mix well.

Assembling the Lasagna:

Preheat Oven:
- Preheat your oven to 375°F (190°C).

Layering:
- In a baking dish, spread a thin layer of the meat sauce. Place three cooked lasagna noodles on top. Spread half of the ricotta mixture over the noodles, followed by a layer of shredded mozzarella cheese. Repeat the layers, ending with a layer of meat sauce and mozzarella cheese on top.

Cover and Bake:
- Cover the baking dish with aluminum foil and bake in the preheated oven for 30 minutes.

Uncover and Bake:
- Remove the foil and bake for an additional 10-15 minutes or until the cheese is melted and bubbly.

Rest Before Serving:
- Allow the Turkey Lasagna to rest for about 10 minutes before slicing.

Garnish and Serve:
- Garnish with fresh basil leaves if desired. Slice and serve your delicious Turkey Lasagna.

This turkey lasagna is a comforting and satisfying dish that can be enjoyed by the whole family. Feel free to customize it by adding your favorite vegetables or adjusting the seasonings according to your taste.

Seafood Recipes:

Grilled Shrimp Skewers

Ingredients:

- 1 pound large shrimp, peeled and deveined
- 2 tablespoons olive oil
- 2 cloves garlic, minced
- 1 teaspoon smoked paprika
- 1 teaspoon dried oregano
- 1/2 teaspoon cumin
- 1/2 teaspoon red pepper flakes (adjust to taste)
- Salt and black pepper to taste
- 1 lemon, juiced
- Wooden or metal skewers

Instructions:

Prepare Shrimp:
- If using wooden skewers, soak them in water for about 30 minutes to prevent burning. Pat the shrimp dry with paper towels.

Marinate Shrimp:
- In a bowl, combine olive oil, minced garlic, smoked paprika, dried oregano, cumin, red pepper flakes, salt, black pepper, and lemon juice. Mix well. Add the shrimp to the marinade and toss to coat evenly. Let it marinate for 15-30 minutes.

Preheat Grill:
- Preheat your grill to medium-high heat.

Skewer Shrimp:
- Thread the marinated shrimp onto skewers, ensuring they are evenly spaced.

Grill Shrimp:
- Place the shrimp skewers on the preheated grill. Grill for 2-3 minutes per side or until the shrimp are opaque and have grill marks.

Baste with Marinade (Optional):
- If desired, you can baste the shrimp with the remaining marinade during the last minute of grilling for extra flavor.

Serve:

- Remove the shrimp skewers from the grill and transfer them to a serving plate.

Garnish and Enjoy:
- Garnish with fresh chopped parsley and serve immediately. Enjoy your Grilled Shrimp Skewers!

These grilled shrimp skewers are versatile and can be served as an appetizer, main dish, or added to salads. Feel free to customize the marinade with your favorite herbs and spices. They are quick to make and full of delicious, smoky flavors.

Lemon Garlic Butter Salmon

Ingredients:

- 4 salmon fillets
- Salt and black pepper to taste
- 2 tablespoons olive oil
- 4 cloves garlic, minced
- 1/4 cup chicken or vegetable broth
- Juice of 1 lemon
- Zest of 1 lemon
- 2 tablespoons unsalted butter
- Fresh parsley, chopped, for garnish
- Lemon slices for serving

Instructions:

Preheat Oven:
- Preheat your oven to 400°F (200°C).

Season Salmon:
- Pat the salmon fillets dry with paper towels. Season them with salt and black pepper on both sides.

Sear Salmon:
- In an oven-safe skillet, heat olive oil over medium-high heat. Place the salmon fillets in the skillet, skin side down, and sear for 2-3 minutes until golden brown.

Flip Salmon:
- Carefully flip the salmon fillets with a spatula, so the skin side is now facing up.

Add Garlic:
- Add minced garlic to the skillet and cook for about 1 minute until fragrant.

Deglaze with Broth:
- Pour in the chicken or vegetable broth to deglaze the skillet, scraping up any browned bits from the bottom.

Add Lemon Juice and Zest:
- Squeeze the juice of one lemon over the salmon and add the lemon zest.

Bake in the Oven:
- Transfer the skillet to the preheated oven and bake for 10-12 minutes or until the salmon is cooked through and flakes easily with a fork.

Finish with Butter:

- In the last few minutes of baking, add small pieces of butter to the top of each salmon fillet.

Garnish and Serve:
- Remove the skillet from the oven, garnish with chopped parsley, and serve the Lemon Garlic Butter Salmon hot. Optionally, serve with lemon slices on the side.

Enjoy:
- Enjoy your flavorful and juicy Lemon Garlic Butter Salmon!

This dish is not only tasty but also quick to prepare, making it a perfect choice for a weeknight dinner. The combination of lemon, garlic, and butter enhances the natural richness of the salmon.

Shrimp Scampi

Ingredients:

- 1 pound large shrimp, peeled and deveined
- Salt and black pepper to taste
- 8 oz linguine or spaghetti
- 3 tablespoons unsalted butter
- 3 tablespoons olive oil
- 4 cloves garlic, minced
- 1/2 teaspoon red pepper flakes (optional, for heat)
- 1/4 cup chicken broth or white wine
- Juice of 1 lemon
- Zest of 1 lemon
- 1/4 cup fresh parsley, chopped
- Grated Parmesan cheese for serving

Instructions:

Prepare Shrimp:
- Pat the shrimp dry with paper towels and season with salt and black pepper.

Cook Pasta:
- Cook the linguine or spaghetti according to the package instructions. Drain and set aside.

Sauté Shrimp:
- In a large skillet, heat 2 tablespoons of butter and 2 tablespoons of olive oil over medium-high heat. Add the seasoned shrimp and cook for 1-2 minutes per side until they turn pink. Remove the shrimp from the skillet and set aside.

Make Sauce:
- In the same skillet, add the remaining 1 tablespoon of butter and 1 tablespoon of olive oil. Add minced garlic and red pepper flakes (if using) and sauté for about 1 minute until fragrant.

Deglaze with Broth or Wine:
- Pour in chicken broth or white wine to deglaze the skillet, scraping up any browned bits from the bottom.

Add Lemon Juice and Zest:
- Stir in the lemon juice and lemon zest, allowing the flavors to meld for 1-2 minutes.

Combine with Shrimp and Pasta:
- Return the cooked shrimp to the skillet, add the cooked pasta, and toss everything together until well coated in the sauce.

Finish with Parsley:
- Stir in chopped fresh parsley, reserving some for garnish.

Serve:
- Plate the Shrimp Scampi, garnish with additional parsley, and serve hot.

Optional: Parmesan Cheese:
- Sprinkle grated Parmesan cheese over each serving if desired.

Enjoy:
- Enjoy your delicious and aromatic Shrimp Scampi!

This dish is a perfect combination of garlic, butter, and lemon that enhances the natural sweetness of the shrimp. Serve it with a side of crusty bread or a simple green salad for a complete meal.

Crab Cakes

Ingredients:

- 1 pound lump crab meat, picked over for shells
- 1/2 cup breadcrumbs
- 1/4 cup mayonnaise
- 1 large egg, beaten
- 1 tablespoon Dijon mustard
- 1 tablespoon Worcestershire sauce
- 1 tablespoon fresh lemon juice
- 1 teaspoon Old Bay seasoning (or seafood seasoning)
- 1/4 cup finely chopped fresh parsley
- Salt and black pepper to taste
- 1/4 cup vegetable oil (for frying)

Instructions:

Prepare Crab Cakes Mixture:
- In a large bowl, gently combine lump crab meat, breadcrumbs, mayonnaise, beaten egg, Dijon mustard, Worcestershire sauce, fresh lemon juice, Old Bay seasoning, chopped parsley, salt, and black pepper. Be careful not to break up the crab meat too much.

Form Crab Cakes:
- Divide the mixture into equal portions and shape them into crab cakes. You can make them as large or small as you prefer.

Chill the Crab Cakes:
- Place the formed crab cakes on a baking sheet lined with parchment paper and refrigerate for at least 30 minutes. Chilling helps the crab cakes hold their shape during cooking.

Heat Oil:
- In a large skillet, heat vegetable oil over medium-high heat.

Cook Crab Cakes:
- Carefully place the chilled crab cakes in the skillet and cook for 3-4 minutes per side, or until they are golden brown and heated through. Be gentle when flipping to avoid breaking them.

Drain on Paper Towels:
- Once cooked, transfer the crab cakes to a plate lined with paper towels to absorb any excess oil.

Serve:

- Serve the crab cakes hot with your favorite dipping sauce or a squeeze of fresh lemon.

Garnish (Optional):

- Garnish with additional fresh parsley or lemon wedges if desired.

Enjoy:

- Enjoy your delicious and homemade Crab Cakes!

These crab cakes are perfect as an appetizer or as a main course. Pair them with a side salad, coleslaw, or a simple remoulade sauce for a delightful meal.

Fish Tacos with Chipotle Mayo

Ingredients:

For the Chipotle Mayo:

- 1/2 cup mayonnaise
- 1-2 tablespoons adobo sauce from a can of chipotle peppers
- 1 tablespoon lime juice
- Salt to taste

For the Fish Tacos:

- 1 pound white fish fillets (cod, tilapia, or your choice)
- 1 cup all-purpose flour
- 1 teaspoon chili powder
- 1/2 teaspoon cumin
- 1/2 teaspoon garlic powder
- Salt and black pepper to taste
- 1 cup buttermilk (or milk)
- Vegetable oil for frying
- 8 small flour or corn tortillas
- Shredded cabbage or lettuce
- Fresh cilantro, chopped
- Lime wedges for serving

Instructions:

For the Chipotle Mayo:

Prepare Chipotle Mayo:
- In a bowl, whisk together mayonnaise, adobo sauce, lime juice, and salt. Adjust the amount of adobo sauce according to your spice preference. Refrigerate until ready to use.

For the Fish Tacos:

Prepare Fish Fillets:
- Pat the fish fillets dry with paper towels. Cut them into manageable-sized pieces.

Prepare Batter:

- In a shallow bowl, whisk together flour, chili powder, cumin, garlic powder, salt, and black pepper. Pour buttermilk into another bowl.

Coat Fish in Batter:
- Dip each piece of fish into the flour mixture, coating it evenly. Shake off any excess flour. Then, dip it into the buttermilk, allowing any excess to drip off.

Fry Fish:
- In a large skillet, heat vegetable oil over medium-high heat. Fry the fish pieces for 2-3 minutes per side, or until they are golden brown and cooked through. Place them on a paper towel-lined plate to absorb any excess oil.

Warm Tortillas:
- Warm the tortillas according to the package instructions or on a hot skillet for a few seconds on each side.

Assemble Tacos:
- Spread a spoonful of chipotle mayo onto each tortilla. Place a piece of fried fish on top. Top with shredded cabbage or lettuce, chopped cilantro, and a squeeze of lime juice.

Serve:
- Serve the Fish Tacos with Chipotle Mayo immediately.

Enjoy:
- Enjoy these delicious fish tacos with the perfect balance of crispy, spicy, and creamy flavors!

These fish tacos are customizable, so feel free to add your favorite toppings like diced tomatoes, avocado slices, or pickled onions. They make for a fantastic and satisfying meal.

Baked Cod with Herbs

Ingredients:

- 4 cod fillets (about 6 ounces each)
- Salt and black pepper to taste
- 2 tablespoons olive oil
- 2 tablespoons fresh parsley, chopped
- 1 tablespoon fresh dill, chopped
- 1 tablespoon fresh chives, chopped
- 2 cloves garlic, minced
- Zest of 1 lemon
- 1 tablespoon lemon juice
- Lemon wedges for serving

Instructions:

Preheat Oven:
- Preheat your oven to 400°F (200°C).

Prepare Cod Fillets:
- Pat the cod fillets dry with paper towels. Season both sides with salt and black pepper.

Mix Herb Mixture:
- In a small bowl, combine chopped parsley, dill, chives, minced garlic, lemon zest, and lemon juice. Add olive oil and mix well to create a herb mixture.

Coat Cod with Herb Mixture:
- Place the cod fillets on a baking dish lined with parchment paper. Coat the fillets evenly with the herb mixture, pressing it gently onto the fish.

Bake:
- Bake in the preheated oven for 12-15 minutes, or until the cod is opaque and flakes easily with a fork.

Serve:
- Remove the baked cod from the oven and serve hot.

Garnish and Enjoy:
- Garnish with additional fresh herbs, if desired, and serve with lemon wedges. Enjoy your Baked Cod with Herbs!

This dish is not only healthy and light but also packed with fresh flavors from the herbs and lemon. Serve it alongside steamed vegetables, a simple salad, or your favorite side dishes for a well-rounded meal.

Garlic Butter Lobster Tails

Ingredients:

- 4 lobster tails
- Salt and black pepper to taste
- 1/2 cup unsalted butter, melted
- 4 cloves garlic, minced
- 1 tablespoon fresh parsley, chopped
- 1 tablespoon fresh lemon juice
- Lemon wedges for serving

Instructions:

Preheat Oven:
- Preheat your oven to 425°F (220°C).

Prepare Lobster Tails:
- Using kitchen shears, cut through the top shell of each lobster tail, stopping at the tail fan. Use your fingers to gently open the shell, exposing the lobster meat.

Season Lobster Tails:
- Season the lobster tails with salt and black pepper to taste.

Garlic Butter Mixture:
- In a small bowl, mix together melted butter, minced garlic, chopped parsley, and lemon juice.

Brush Lobster Tails:
- Brush the exposed lobster meat with the garlic butter mixture, ensuring it gets into the shell and over the meat.

Arrange on Baking Sheet:
- Place the prepared lobster tails on a baking sheet lined with parchment paper or aluminum foil.

Bake:
- Bake in the preheated oven for about 12-15 minutes or until the lobster meat is opaque and cooked through. The shells will turn bright red.

Baste:
- While baking, baste the lobster tails with the garlic butter mixture every 5 minutes to keep them moist and flavorful.

Serve:
- Once done, remove the lobster tails from the oven.

Garnish and Enjoy:

- Garnish with additional chopped parsley and serve the garlic butter lobster tails hot with lemon wedges on the side.

These garlic butter lobster tails are perfect for a special occasion or a romantic dinner. Serve them with your favorite side dishes or a simple salad to complement the rich and savory flavors.

Clam Linguine

Ingredients:

- 8 ounces linguine
- 2 tablespoons olive oil
- 4 cloves garlic, minced
- 1/2 teaspoon red pepper flakes (optional, for heat)
- 1 cup dry white wine
- 2 dozen littleneck clams, scrubbed and cleaned
- Salt and black pepper to taste
- 1/4 cup fresh parsley, chopped
- 2 tablespoons unsalted butter
- Grated Parmesan cheese for serving (optional)
- Lemon wedges for serving

Instructions:

Cook Linguine:
- Cook the linguine in a large pot of salted boiling water according to the package instructions until al dente. Reserve a cup of pasta cooking water and then drain the linguine.

Prepare Clams:
- In a large skillet, heat olive oil over medium heat. Add minced garlic and red pepper flakes (if using) and sauté for about 1 minute until fragrant.

Add White Wine:
- Pour in the white wine and bring it to a simmer. Let it cook for 2-3 minutes to allow the alcohol to evaporate.

Cook Clams:
- Add the cleaned clams to the skillet, cover, and cook for 5-7 minutes, or until the clams open. Discard any clams that do not open.

Season:
- Season the sauce with salt and black pepper to taste. Keep in mind that the clam liquor is naturally salty, so be cautious with the additional salt.

Add Linguine:
- Add the cooked linguine to the skillet and toss everything together. If the sauce is too dry, add a bit of the reserved pasta cooking water.

Finish with Butter and Parsley:
- Stir in unsalted butter and chopped fresh parsley. Toss until the linguine is well coated.

Serve:
- Divide the Clam Linguine among plates. If desired, sprinkle with grated Parmesan cheese and serve with lemon wedges on the side.

Enjoy:
- Enjoy your delicious and flavorful Clam Linguine!

This dish is a celebration of the sea's flavors, and the briny taste of the clams pairs wonderfully with the garlic-infused white wine sauce. It's a perfect choice for seafood lovers and those who appreciate a taste of Italy in their pasta.

Seafood Paella

Ingredients:

- 1 1/2 cups bomba rice (or short-grain rice)
- 4 cups chicken broth (or fish stock)
- 1/2 teaspoon saffron threads
- 1/4 cup olive oil
- 1 onion, finely chopped
- 4 cloves garlic, minced
- 1 red bell pepper, thinly sliced
- 1 yellow bell pepper, thinly sliced
- 1 tomato, diced
- 1 teaspoon smoked paprika
- 1/2 teaspoon cayenne pepper (optional, for heat)
- 1 cup dry white wine
- 1 pound mixed seafood (e.g., shrimp, mussels, squid, clams)
- Salt and black pepper to taste
- Fresh parsley, chopped, for garnish
- Lemon wedges for serving

Instructions:

Prepare Saffron Broth:
- In a small bowl, warm the chicken broth and steep the saffron threads in it. Allow it to infuse while you prepare the other ingredients.

Sauté Vegetables:
- In a large paella pan or a wide skillet, heat olive oil over medium heat. Add chopped onion and sauté until softened. Add minced garlic and continue to sauté for another minute.

Add Peppers and Tomato:
- Stir in the sliced red and yellow bell peppers and diced tomato. Cook until the vegetables are softened.

Season with Paprika and Cayenne:
- Sprinkle smoked paprika and cayenne pepper (if using) over the vegetables. Stir to coat evenly.

Add Rice:
- Add the bomba rice to the pan and stir, allowing the rice to absorb the flavors of the vegetables and spices.

Pour in White Wine:

- Pour in the dry white wine and let it simmer for a couple of minutes, allowing the alcohol to evaporate.

Pour Saffron Broth:
- Strain the saffron threads from the warmed chicken broth and pour the saffron-infused broth over the rice.

Arrange Seafood:
- Arrange the mixed seafood evenly over the rice. Press the seafood into the rice but avoid stirring from this point forward.

Simmer and Cook:
- Reduce the heat to low and simmer until the rice is cooked and has formed a crust on the bottom (socarrat), and the seafood is cooked through. This takes about 15-20 minutes.

Season and Garnish:
- Season with salt and black pepper to taste. Garnish with chopped fresh parsley.

Serve:
- Serve the Seafood Paella directly from the pan, garnished with lemon wedges.

Enjoy:
- Enjoy your delicious and authentic Seafood Paella!

This dish is a festive and communal meal, perfect for gatherings. The saffron-infused rice and the combination of seafood create a rich and flavorful experience.

Teriyaki Glazed Grilled Swordfish

Ingredients:

For the Teriyaki Glaze:

- 1/2 cup soy sauce
- 1/4 cup mirin
- 2 tablespoons sake (or white wine)
- 2 tablespoons brown sugar
- 2 cloves garlic, minced
- 1 teaspoon ginger, grated
- 1 tablespoon cornstarch (optional, for thickening)

For the Grilled Swordfish:

- 4 swordfish steaks (about 6-8 ounces each)
- Salt and black pepper to taste
- 2 tablespoons vegetable oil
- Sesame seeds for garnish (optional)
- Chopped green onions for garnish (optional)

Instructions:

For the Teriyaki Glaze:

> Mix Ingredients:
> - In a small saucepan, combine soy sauce, mirin, sake (or white wine), brown sugar, minced garlic, and grated ginger.
>
> Bring to a Simmer:
> - Heat the mixture over medium heat, stirring to dissolve the sugar. Bring it to a simmer.
>
> Optional Thickening:
> - If you prefer a thicker glaze, mix cornstarch with a little water to make a slurry. Stir the slurry into the sauce and simmer until it thickens. Remove from heat and let it cool.

For the Grilled Swordfish:

> Preheat Grill:
> - Preheat your grill to medium-high heat.
>
> Prepare Swordfish:

- Pat the swordfish steaks dry with paper towels. Season them with salt and black pepper to taste.

Brush with Oil:
- Brush the swordfish steaks with vegetable oil to prevent sticking to the grill.

Grill Swordfish:
- Place the swordfish steaks on the preheated grill. Grill for about 4-5 minutes per side, or until the fish is cooked through and has nice grill marks.

Brush with Teriyaki Glaze:
- Brush the teriyaki glaze generously over the swordfish during the last few minutes of grilling.

Garnish:
- Remove the swordfish from the grill, garnish with sesame seeds and chopped green onions if desired.

Serve:
- Serve the Teriyaki Glazed Grilled Swordfish hot.

Enjoy:
- Enjoy the delicious combination of teriyaki-glazed swordfish with a perfect balance of sweet and savory flavors!

This dish pairs well with steamed rice or grilled vegetables. The teriyaki glaze adds a delightful layer of flavor to the grilled swordfish, making it a wonderful choice for a flavorful and satisfying meal.

Miscellaneous Meat Recipes:
Meatball Subs

Ingredients:

For the Meatballs:

- 1 pound ground beef (or a mixture of beef and pork)
- 1/2 cup breadcrumbs
- 1/4 cup grated Parmesan cheese
- 1/4 cup chopped fresh parsley
- 2 cloves garlic, minced
- 1 large egg
- Salt and black pepper to taste
- Olive oil for frying

For the Marinara Sauce:

- 2 cups tomato sauce
- 1 teaspoon dried oregano
- 1 teaspoon dried basil
- 1/2 teaspoon garlic powder
- Salt and black pepper to taste

For the Subs:

- Hoagie or sub rolls
- Shredded mozzarella cheese
- Fresh basil or parsley for garnish (optional)

Instructions:

For the Meatballs:

   Preheat Oven:
   - Preheat your oven to 375°F (190°C).

   Mix Meatball Ingredients:
   - In a large bowl, combine ground beef, breadcrumbs, grated Parmesan cheese, chopped fresh parsley, minced garlic, egg, salt, and black pepper. Mix until well combined.

   Form Meatballs:

- Shape the mixture into meatballs, about 1 to 1.5 inches in diameter.

Fry Meatballs:
- In a skillet, heat olive oil over medium heat. Fry the meatballs until browned on all sides. They don't need to be fully cooked at this stage.

Make Marinara Sauce:
- In a separate saucepan, combine tomato sauce, dried oregano, dried basil, garlic powder, salt, and black pepper. Simmer over low heat.

Bake Meatballs:
- Place the partially cooked meatballs into the simmering marinara sauce. Cover the saucepan and transfer it to the preheated oven. Bake for 15-20 minutes, or until the meatballs are fully cooked.

For Assembling the Subs:

Prepare Sub Rolls:
- Slice the hoagie or sub rolls lengthwise, leaving one side attached.

Add Meatballs and Sauce:
- Place a few meatballs with marinara sauce into each sub roll.

Top with Cheese:
- Sprinkle shredded mozzarella cheese over the meatballs.

Broil:
- Place the meatball subs under the broiler for 2-3 minutes, or until the cheese is melted and bubbly.

Garnish:
- Garnish with fresh basil or parsley if desired.

Serve:
- Serve the Meatball Subs hot.

Enjoy:
- Enjoy these delicious and cheesy Meatball Subs!

These subs make for a hearty and satisfying meal. Serve them with a side of coleslaw, potato chips, or a simple green salad for a complete and comforting experience.

Stuffed Bell Peppers with Ground Meat

Ingredients:

- 4 large bell peppers, any color
- 1 pound ground beef or a mixture of beef and pork
- 1 cup cooked rice (white or brown)
- 1 onion, finely chopped
- 2 cloves garlic, minced
- 1 can (14 oz) diced tomatoes, drained
- 1 cup tomato sauce
- 1 teaspoon dried oregano
- 1 teaspoon dried basil
- Salt and black pepper to taste
- 1 cup shredded mozzarella cheese (optional)
- Fresh parsley or basil for garnish (optional)

Instructions:

Preheat Oven:
- Preheat your oven to 375°F (190°C).

Prepare Bell Peppers:
- Cut the tops off the bell peppers and remove the seeds and membranes. If needed, trim the bottoms of the peppers to make them stand upright in the baking dish.

Parboil Bell Peppers:
- Bring a large pot of water to a boil. Add the bell peppers and cook for 3-5 minutes to parboil them. This step helps soften the peppers before baking. Drain and set aside.

Cook Ground Meat:
- In a skillet, cook the ground beef (or beef and pork mixture) over medium heat until browned. Drain excess fat if necessary.

Sauté Onion and Garlic:
- Add chopped onion and minced garlic to the skillet with the cooked meat. Sauté until the onion is softened.

Combine with Rice and Tomatoes:
- In the skillet, add the cooked rice, drained diced tomatoes, dried oregano, dried basil, salt, and black pepper. Stir to combine.

Fill Bell Peppers:

- Stuff each bell pepper with the meat and rice mixture, pressing it down gently.

Top with Tomato Sauce:
- Pour tomato sauce over the stuffed peppers, ensuring they are generously coated.

Bake:
- Place the stuffed bell peppers in a baking dish. Cover with aluminum foil and bake in the preheated oven for 25-30 minutes.

Optional Cheese Topping:
- If desired, remove the foil, sprinkle shredded mozzarella cheese over each stuffed pepper, and bake for an additional 5-7 minutes or until the cheese is melted and bubbly.

Garnish and Serve:
- Garnish with fresh parsley or basil if desired. Serve the Stuffed Bell Peppers hot.

Enjoy:
- Enjoy these flavorful and comforting Stuffed Bell Peppers!

These stuffed bell peppers make a wholesome and satisfying meal. Pair them with a side salad or your favorite condiments for a delicious and complete dinner.

Meat Lover's Pizza

Ingredients:

For the Pizza Dough:

- 1 pound pizza dough (store-bought or homemade)

For the Pizza Sauce:

- 1 cup pizza sauce

For the Toppings:

- 1/2 cup sliced pepperoni
- 1/2 cup cooked and crumbled Italian sausage
- 1/2 cup cooked and crumbled bacon
- 1/2 cup sliced cooked ham
- 1/2 cup sliced cooked chicken (optional)
- 1 cup shredded mozzarella cheese
- 1/2 cup shredded cheddar cheese
- 1/4 cup grated Parmesan cheese
- Crushed red pepper flakes (optional, for added heat)
- Fresh basil or parsley for garnish (optional)

Instructions:

Preheat Oven:
- Preheat your oven to the temperature specified on the pizza dough package or your homemade dough recipe.

Roll Out Pizza Dough:
- Roll out the pizza dough on a lightly floured surface to your desired thickness.

Prepare Pizza Stone or Pan:
- If using a pizza stone, place it in the oven to heat. If using a pizza pan, lightly grease it.

Transfer Dough:
- Carefully transfer the rolled-out dough to the preheated pizza stone or pan.

Spread Pizza Sauce:
- Spread the pizza sauce evenly over the dough, leaving a small border around the edges.

Add Toppings:
- Distribute the sliced pepperoni, crumbled Italian sausage, crumbled bacon, sliced ham, and sliced chicken (if using) evenly over the pizza.

Sprinkle Cheese:
- Sprinkle the shredded mozzarella, cheddar, and grated Parmesan cheese over the toppings.

Optional Heat:
- If you like it spicy, sprinkle some crushed red pepper flakes over the pizza.

Bake:
- Bake the Meat Lover's Pizza in the preheated oven according to the dough instructions or until the crust is golden and the cheese is melted and bubbly.

Garnish and Serve:
- Once out of the oven, garnish with fresh basil or parsley if desired.

Slice and Enjoy:
- Slice the pizza and enjoy your Meat Lover's Pizza while it's hot!

This Meat Lover's Pizza is customizable, so feel free to add or omit toppings based on your preferences. Serve it with a side salad for a complete meal or enjoy it on its own as a satisfying and indulgent treat.

Empanadas with Ground Meat

Ingredients:

For the Dough:

- 3 cups all-purpose flour
- 1 teaspoon salt
- 1 cup unsalted butter, cold and cut into small pieces
- 1/2 cup cold water

For the Filling:

- 1 tablespoon vegetable oil
- 1 onion, finely chopped
- 2 cloves garlic, minced
- 1 pound ground beef or a mixture of beef and pork
- 1 teaspoon ground cumin
- 1 teaspoon paprika
- 1/2 teaspoon dried oregano
- Salt and black pepper to taste
- 1/2 cup green olives, chopped
- 1/4 cup raisins
- 2 hard-boiled eggs, chopped

For Assembly and Baking:

- 1 egg (for egg wash)
- 2 tablespoons water (for egg wash)
- Sesame seeds or poppy seeds (optional, for sprinkling)

Instructions:

For the Dough:

Prepare Dough:
- In a large bowl, combine the flour and salt. Add the cold, diced butter and use your fingers or a pastry cutter to work it into the flour until the mixture resembles coarse crumbs.

Add Water:

- Gradually add cold water, mixing until the dough comes together. Form the dough into a ball, wrap it in plastic wrap, and refrigerate for at least 30 minutes.

For the Filling:

Sauté Onion and Garlic:
- In a skillet, heat vegetable oil over medium heat. Sauté chopped onion and minced garlic until softened.

Cook Ground Meat:
- Add ground beef (or beef and pork mixture) to the skillet and cook until browned. Drain any excess fat.

Season:
- Add ground cumin, paprika, dried oregano, salt, and black pepper to the meat mixture. Stir to combine.

Add Olives, Raisins, and Eggs:
- Mix in chopped green olives, raisins, and chopped hard-boiled eggs. Remove the filling from heat and let it cool.

For Assembly and Baking:

Preheat Oven:
- Preheat your oven to 375°F (190°C).

Roll Out Dough:
- On a floured surface, roll out the chilled dough to about 1/8 inch thickness.

Cut Dough Circles:
- Use a round cutter or a glass to cut circles from the rolled-out dough.

Add Filling:
- Place a spoonful of the cooled meat filling in the center of each dough circle.

Fold and Seal:
- Fold the dough over the filling to create a half-moon shape. Seal the edges by pressing with a fork.

Egg Wash:
- In a small bowl, whisk together an egg and water to make an egg wash. Brush the empanadas with the egg wash.

Sprinkle Seeds (Optional):
- If desired, sprinkle sesame seeds or poppy seeds over the top of the empanadas.

Bake:

- Place the empanadas on a baking sheet lined with parchment paper. Bake in the preheated oven for 20-25 minutes or until golden brown.

Cool and Enjoy:
- Allow the empanadas to cool slightly before serving. Enjoy your delicious Empanadas with Ground Meat!

These empanadas are great for a snack, appetizer, or even a main course. Serve them with a dipping sauce or enjoy them as is for a tasty and satisfying treat.

Beef and Sausage Lasagna

Ingredients:

For the Meat Sauce:

- 1 pound ground beef
- 1/2 pound Italian sausage, casings removed
- 1 onion, finely chopped
- 3 cloves garlic, minced
- 1 can (28 oz) crushed tomatoes
- 1 can (15 oz) tomato sauce
- 1 can (6 oz) tomato paste
- 1/2 cup red wine (optional)
- 2 teaspoons dried oregano
- 1 teaspoon dried basil
- 1/2 teaspoon sugar
- Salt and black pepper to taste

For the Ricotta Mixture:

- 2 cups ricotta cheese
- 1 cup shredded mozzarella cheese
- 1/2 cup grated Parmesan cheese
- 2 large eggs
- 2 tablespoons fresh parsley, chopped
- Salt and black pepper to taste

Other Ingredients:

- 9 lasagna noodles, cooked according to package instructions
- 2 cups shredded mozzarella cheese
- 1/2 cup grated Parmesan cheese

Instructions:

For the Meat Sauce:

    Cook Ground Meat:
- In a large pot or skillet, cook the ground beef and Italian sausage over medium heat until browned. Break the meat into small pieces with a spatula.

    Sauté Onion and Garlic:

- Add chopped onion and minced garlic to the pot. Sauté until the onion is softened.

Add Tomatoes and Sauce:
- Stir in crushed tomatoes, tomato sauce, and tomato paste. Mix well.

Season and Simmer:
- Add red wine (if using), dried oregano, dried basil, sugar, salt, and black pepper. Bring the sauce to a simmer and let it cook for at least 30 minutes, allowing the flavors to meld. Adjust seasoning if necessary.

For the Ricotta Mixture:

Prepare Ricotta Mixture:
- In a bowl, combine ricotta cheese, shredded mozzarella cheese, grated Parmesan cheese, eggs, chopped parsley, salt, and black pepper. Mix until well combined.

For Assembly:

Preheat Oven:
- Preheat your oven to 375°F (190°C).

Assemble Lasagna:
- In a baking dish, spread a thin layer of the meat sauce. Place three cooked lasagna noodles on top.

Layer Ricotta Mixture:
- Spread half of the ricotta mixture over the noodles.

Add Meat Sauce and Cheese:
- Add a layer of meat sauce on top of the ricotta mixture. Sprinkle with shredded mozzarella and grated Parmesan.

Repeat Layers:
- Repeat the layers with the remaining noodles, ricotta mixture, meat sauce, and cheeses.

Final Layer:
- Finish with a layer of meat sauce and a generous sprinkle of shredded mozzarella and grated Parmesan.

Bake:
- Cover the baking dish with foil and bake in the preheated oven for 25 minutes. Then, remove the foil and bake for an additional 15-20 minutes or until the cheese is melted and bubbly, and the edges are golden.

Rest and Serve:
- Let the lasagna rest for about 10 minutes before slicing. Serve warm.

Enjoy:
- Enjoy your delicious Beef and Sausage Lasagna!

This lasagna is a crowd-pleaser and perfect for gatherings. Serve it with a side salad and some garlic bread for a complete and comforting meal.

Kebabs with Mixed Meats

Ingredients:

For the Marinade:

- 1/4 cup olive oil
- 2 tablespoons plain yogurt
- 3 cloves garlic, minced
- 1 teaspoon ground cumin
- 1 teaspoon ground coriander
- 1 teaspoon paprika
- 1 teaspoon dried oregano
- Salt and black pepper to taste
- Juice of 1 lemon

For the Kebabs:

- 1 pound boneless, skinless chicken breast, cut into bite-sized chunks
- 1 pound beef sirloin or lamb, cut into bite-sized chunks
- 1/2 pound pork tenderloin, cut into bite-sized chunks
- Assorted vegetables for skewering (bell peppers, onions, cherry tomatoes, zucchini, mushrooms, etc.)
- Wooden or metal skewers (if using wooden skewers, soak them in water for about 30 minutes before using)

Instructions:

Prepare Marinade:
- In a bowl, whisk together olive oil, yogurt, minced garlic, ground cumin, ground coriander, paprika, dried oregano, salt, black pepper, and lemon juice.

Marinate Meats:
- Place the chicken, beef (or lamb), and pork chunks into the marinade. Ensure the meats are well-coated. Cover the bowl and let it marinate in the refrigerator for at least 1-2 hours, or overnight for the best flavor.

Preheat Grill:
- Preheat your grill to medium-high heat.

Assemble Kebabs:
- Thread the marinated meat chunks onto skewers, alternating with assorted vegetables.

Brush with Marinade:
- Before placing the kebabs on the grill, brush them with a bit of the remaining marinade.

Grill Kebabs:
- Grill the kebabs for about 10-15 minutes, turning occasionally, until the meats are cooked through and have a nice char on the outside.

Serve Hot:
- Remove the kebabs from the grill and let them rest for a few minutes. Serve the mixed meat kebabs hot.

Optional:
- Garnish with chopped fresh herbs like parsley or cilantro before serving.

Enjoy:
- Enjoy these delicious mixed meat kebabs on their own or with a side of rice, couscous, or a fresh salad.

Feel free to customize the marinade and choose your favorite combination of meats and vegetables. These kebabs are perfect for a barbecue or outdoor gathering, and they're sure to be a hit with family and friends.

Meat and Cheese Platter

Ingredients:

For the Meats:

- Prosciutto: Thinly sliced Italian cured ham.
- Salami: Different varieties such as Genoa, Soppressata, or Chorizo.
- Roast Beef: Sliced thin for a savory option.
- Turkey or Chicken: Smoked or roasted slices.

For the Cheeses:

- Brie: Creamy and mild.
- Cheddar: Sharp and firm.
- Gouda: Smoked or aged for a distinct flavor.
- Blue Cheese: Creamy and pungent.
- Manchego: A Spanish sheep's milk cheese.
- Goat Cheese: Tangy and spreadable.

Accompaniments:

- Crackers: Assorted types, including plain, whole grain, and flavored.
- Bread: Sliced baguette or artisanal bread.
- Fresh Fruits: Grapes, apple slices, or figs.
- Dried Fruits: Apricots, figs, or dates.
- Nuts: Almonds, walnuts, or pecans.
- Olives: Green and black varieties.
- Honey or Fig Jam: For drizzling over cheese.

Garnishes:

- Fresh Herbs: Rosemary, thyme, or basil.
- Edible Flowers: For a decorative touch.

Instructions:

Select a Platter or Board:
- Choose a large platter or wooden board to arrange your meats and cheeses.

Arrange Cheeses:
- Place the cheeses on the board, leaving enough space between them. Consider different shapes and sizes for visual appeal.

Arrange Meats:
- Artfully arrange the various meats around the cheeses. Overlapping or folding slices can create an attractive display.

Add Crackers and Bread:
- Place an assortment of crackers and sliced bread in between and around the meats and cheeses.

Incorporate Fresh and Dried Fruits:
- Scatter fresh grapes, apple slices, or figs around the board. Add dried apricots, figs, or dates for sweetness.

Include Nuts and Olives:
- Distribute a variety of nuts like almonds, walnuts, or pecans. Add green and black olives for a savory touch.

Drizzle with Honey or Jam:
- Place small bowls of honey or fig jam on the board for dipping or drizzling over the cheeses.

Garnish:
- Garnish the platter with fresh herbs like rosemary or thyme. Consider adding edible flowers for an extra decorative touch.

Serve at Room Temperature:
- Allow the cheeses and meats to come to room temperature for the best flavors. This can take about 30 minutes before serving.

Present and Enjoy:
- Present your meat and cheese platter to guests and enjoy the delightful combination of flavors and textures.

Feel free to personalize the platter with your favorite cheeses, meats, and accompaniments. Whether served as an appetizer or part of a larger spread, a well-curated meat and cheese platter is sure to be a hit at any gathering.

Meat Pie

Ingredients:

For the Pastry:

- 2 1/2 cups all-purpose flour
- 1 cup unsalted butter, cold and cut into small cubes
- 1/2 teaspoon salt
- 1/2 cup ice-cold water

For the Filling:

- 1 pound ground beef or a mixture of beef and pork
- 1 onion, finely chopped
- 2 cloves garlic, minced
- 1 carrot, diced
- 1 celery stalk, diced
- 1 cup frozen peas
- 2 tablespoons all-purpose flour
- 1 cup beef or vegetable broth
- 1 tablespoon tomato paste
- 1 teaspoon Worcestershire sauce
- Salt and black pepper to taste
- 1 egg (for egg wash)

Instructions:

For the Pastry:

  Prepare the Dough:
  - In a large bowl, combine the flour and salt. Add the cold, cubed butter. Use a pastry cutter or your fingers to incorporate the butter into the flour until the mixture resembles coarse crumbs.

  Add Water:
  - Gradually add the ice-cold water, a little at a time, and mix until the dough comes together. Form the dough into a ball, wrap it in plastic wrap, and refrigerate for at least 30 minutes.

For the Filling:

Cook Meat:
- In a large skillet, brown the ground beef (or beef and pork mixture) over medium heat. Drain any excess fat.

Add Vegetables:
- Add chopped onion, minced garlic, diced carrot, and diced celery to the skillet. Cook until the vegetables are softened.

Add Flour:
- Sprinkle the flour over the meat and vegetable mixture. Stir well to combine.

Add Broth and Flavorings:
- Pour in the beef or vegetable broth. Add tomato paste, Worcestershire sauce, salt, and black pepper. Stir until the mixture thickens.

Add Peas:
- Stir in the frozen peas and cook for a few more minutes until the peas are heated through. Remove the filling from heat and let it cool.

Assembling the Meat Pie:

Preheat Oven:
- Preheat your oven to 400°F (200°C).

Roll Out Pastry:
- On a floured surface, roll out the chilled pastry dough to fit the bottom and top of your pie dish.

Line Pie Dish:
- Place one rolled-out pastry sheet into the bottom of a pie dish.

Add Filling:
- Spoon the cooled meat and vegetable filling into the pastry-lined dish.

Cover with Pastry:
- Place the second rolled-out pastry sheet on top of the filling. Trim any excess dough and crimp the edges to seal the pie.

Ventilation Holes:
- Use a sharp knife to make a few small ventilation holes in the top pastry crust.

Egg Wash:
- Beat an egg and brush it over the top of the pastry for a golden finish.

Bake:
- Bake in the preheated oven for 30-40 minutes or until the pastry is golden brown and the filling is hot and bubbling.

Cool and Serve:

- Allow the meat pie to cool for a few minutes before slicing. Serve warm and enjoy!

This meat pie is a comforting and satisfying dish. Feel free to customize the filling with your favorite ingredients, herbs, or spices. Serve it with a side salad for a complete meal.

Chili Con Carne

Ingredients:

- 1 pound ground beef
- 1 onion, chopped
- 3 cloves garlic, minced
- 1 bell pepper, diced
- 1 can (14 oz) diced tomatoes
- 1 can (15 oz) kidney beans, drained and rinsed
- 1 can (15 oz) black beans, drained and rinsed
- 2 tablespoons tomato paste
- 2 teaspoons chili powder
- 1 teaspoon ground cumin
- 1 teaspoon paprika
- 1/2 teaspoon dried oregano
- 1/2 teaspoon cayenne pepper (adjust to taste for spiciness)
- Salt and black pepper to taste
- 1 cup beef or vegetable broth
- 2 tablespoons olive oil
- Optional toppings: shredded cheese, sour cream, chopped green onions, cilantro

Instructions:

Cook Ground Beef:
- In a large pot or Dutch oven, heat olive oil over medium heat. Add ground beef and cook until browned, breaking it apart with a spatula as it cooks.

Sauté Vegetables:
- Add chopped onion, minced garlic, and diced bell pepper to the pot. Sauté until the vegetables are softened.

Add Spices:
- Stir in chili powder, ground cumin, paprika, dried oregano, cayenne pepper, salt, and black pepper. Cook for 1-2 minutes to toast the spices.

Incorporate Tomato Paste:
- Add tomato paste to the pot and stir well to combine with the meat and spices.

Add Tomatoes and Beans:
- Pour in the diced tomatoes (with their juices), drained kidney beans, and drained black beans. Mix everything together.

Pour in Broth:

- Pour in the beef or vegetable broth to the pot. Stir to combine all the ingredients.

Simmer:
- Bring the chili to a simmer. Reduce the heat to low, cover the pot, and let it simmer for at least 30 minutes to allow the flavors to meld. You can simmer longer for deeper flavor.

Adjust Seasoning:
- Taste the chili and adjust the seasoning as needed. Add more salt, pepper, or spices if desired.

Serve:
- Ladle the Chili con Carne into bowls. Optionally, top each serving with shredded cheese, a dollop of sour cream, chopped green onions, or cilantro.

Enjoy:
- Serve the chili with your favorite sides, such as cornbread, rice, or tortilla chips. Enjoy the comforting and flavorful Chili con Carne!

This versatile dish is perfect for gatherings, game day, or a comforting weeknight dinner. Adjust the spice levels and toppings to suit your taste preferences.

Carnitas Burritos

Ingredients:

For the Carnitas:

- 2-3 pounds pork shoulder, cut into chunks
- 1 onion, finely chopped
- 4 cloves garlic, minced
- 1 teaspoon ground cumin
- 1 teaspoon dried oregano
- 1 teaspoon smoked paprika
- 1 teaspoon chili powder
- Salt and black pepper to taste
- 1 orange, juiced
- 1 lime, juiced
- 2 tablespoons vegetable oil

For the Burritos:

- Large flour tortillas
- Cooked white or brown rice
- Cooked black beans or pinto beans
- Salsa (store-bought or homemade)
- Guacamole or sliced avocado
- Sour cream
- Shredded lettuce
- Shredded cheese (cheddar, Monterey Jack, or a blend)
- Fresh cilantro, chopped
- Lime wedges for serving

Instructions:

For the Carnitas:

Season Pork:
- In a bowl, combine pork chunks with chopped onion, minced garlic, cumin, oregano, smoked paprika, chili powder, salt, and black pepper.

Marinate:
- Add the juice of one orange and one lime to the pork mixture. Allow the pork to marinate for at least 30 minutes, or refrigerate overnight for more flavor.

Cook Carnitas:

- Heat vegetable oil in a large pot or Dutch oven over medium-high heat. Brown the marinated pork chunks on all sides.

Simmer:
- Pour in the marinade and enough water to cover the pork. Bring it to a boil, then reduce the heat to low, cover, and simmer for 2-3 hours or until the pork is tender and can be easily shredded with a fork.

Shred and Crisp:
- Once the pork is tender, shred it using two forks. If desired, transfer the shredded pork to a baking sheet and broil for a few minutes to crisp up the edges.

Assembling the Carnitas Burritos:

Prepare Burrito Components:
- Warm the flour tortillas. Gather the cooked rice, beans, salsa, guacamole or sliced avocado, sour cream, shredded lettuce, shredded cheese, chopped cilantro, and lime wedges.

Assemble Burritos:
- Lay out a tortilla and add a portion of each component to the center, starting with rice, beans, carnitas, salsa, guacamole or avocado, sour cream, lettuce, cheese, and cilantro.

Fold and Roll:
- Fold the sides of the tortilla over the filling, then fold the bottom up and roll tightly to form a burrito.

Serve:
- Serve the Carnitas Burritos with lime wedges on the side.

Enjoy:
- Enjoy these flavorful and satisfying Carnitas Burritos!

Feel free to customize the burritos with your favorite toppings and adjust the spice levels according to your preference. This recipe is perfect for a delicious and hearty meal that can be enjoyed for lunch or dinner.

Meat and Potato Casserole

Ingredients:

- 1 pound ground beef or ground turkey
- 1 onion, finely chopped
- 2 cloves garlic, minced
- 1 teaspoon dried thyme
- 1 teaspoon dried rosemary
- Salt and black pepper to taste
- 4 cups potatoes, peeled and thinly sliced
- 1 cup frozen peas (optional)
- 1 cup shredded cheddar cheese
- 1 cup beef or vegetable broth
- 2 tablespoons all-purpose flour
- 2 tablespoons tomato paste
- 2 tablespoons Worcestershire sauce
- 2 tablespoons olive oil

Instructions:

Preheat Oven:
- Preheat your oven to 375°F (190°C).

Cook Ground Meat:
- In a skillet over medium heat, cook the ground beef or turkey until browned. Drain any excess fat.

Sauté Onion and Garlic:
- Add chopped onion and minced garlic to the skillet. Sauté until the onion is softened.

Season Meat:
- Season the meat mixture with dried thyme, dried rosemary, salt, and black pepper. Stir to combine.

Add Flour and Tomato Paste:
- Sprinkle the flour over the meat and stir to coat. Add tomato paste and continue stirring for 1-2 minutes.

Pour in Broth and Worcestershire Sauce:
- Pour in the beef or vegetable broth and Worcestershire sauce. Stir well and let it simmer for a few minutes until the mixture thickens. Remove from heat.

Layer Potatoes:

- In a greased baking dish, layer half of the sliced potatoes at the bottom.

Add Meat Mixture:
- Spread half of the meat mixture over the layer of potatoes.

Optional: Add Peas:
- If using frozen peas, sprinkle them over the meat layer.

Repeat Layers:
- Repeat the layers with the remaining potatoes and meat mixture.

Top with Cheese:
- Sprinkle shredded cheddar cheese evenly over the top.

Bake:
- Cover the baking dish with foil and bake in the preheated oven for about 45 minutes. Then, uncover and bake for an additional 15-20 minutes or until the potatoes are tender and the top is golden and bubbly.

Let it Rest:
- Allow the casserole to rest for a few minutes before serving.

Serve:
- Scoop out portions of the Meat and Potato Casserole and serve warm.

This hearty casserole is a complete meal in itself, but you can also serve it with a side salad for a balanced dinner. Feel free to customize the recipe by adding your favorite herbs, spices, or vegetables to suit your taste preferences.

Meatloaf with Tomato Glaze

Ingredients:

For the Meatloaf:

- 1.5 pounds ground beef (or a mixture of beef and pork)
- 1 onion, finely chopped
- 2 cloves garlic, minced
- 1 cup breadcrumbs
- 2 large eggs
- 1/2 cup milk
- 1/4 cup ketchup
- 2 tablespoons Worcestershire sauce
- 1 teaspoon dried thyme
- 1 teaspoon dried oregano
- Salt and black pepper to taste

For the Tomato Glaze:

- 1/2 cup ketchup
- 2 tablespoons brown sugar
- 1 tablespoon Dijon mustard
- 1 teaspoon Worcestershire sauce

Instructions:

Preheat Oven:
- Preheat your oven to 350°F (175°C).

Prepare Meatloaf Mixture:
- In a large mixing bowl, combine ground beef, chopped onion, minced garlic, breadcrumbs, eggs, milk, ketchup, Worcestershire sauce, dried thyme, dried oregano, salt, and black pepper. Mix the ingredients until well combined.

Shape Meatloaf:
- Transfer the meat mixture to a greased or parchment-lined baking dish. Shape it into a loaf.

Prepare Tomato Glaze:
- In a small bowl, whisk together ketchup, brown sugar, Dijon mustard, and Worcestershire sauce to create the glaze.

Apply Tomato Glaze:

- Brush or spread half of the tomato glaze over the top of the meatloaf.

Bake:
- Bake the meatloaf in the preheated oven for approximately 45 minutes.

Apply Remaining Glaze:
- After 45 minutes, remove the meatloaf from the oven and apply the remaining tomato glaze over the top.

Continue Baking:
- Return the meatloaf to the oven and bake for an additional 15-20 minutes or until the internal temperature reaches 160°F (71°C) and the top is nicely caramelized.

Rest:
- Allow the meatloaf to rest for about 10 minutes before slicing.

Slice and Serve:
- Slice the Meatloaf with Tomato Glaze and serve warm.

Optional: Garnish:
- Garnish with fresh herbs like parsley if desired.

This Meatloaf with Tomato Glaze pairs well with mashed potatoes, steamed vegetables, or a side salad. It's a classic, family-friendly dish that's perfect for a comforting dinner.

Greek Moussaka

Ingredients:

For the Eggplant Layer:

- 2 large eggplants, thinly sliced
- Salt
- Olive oil for brushing

For the Meat Filling:

- 1.5 pounds ground lamb or beef
- 1 onion, finely chopped
- 2 cloves garlic, minced
- 1 can (14 oz) crushed tomatoes
- 1 tablespoon tomato paste
- 1 teaspoon dried oregano
- 1 teaspoon ground cinnamon
- Salt and black pepper to taste

For the Béchamel Sauce:

- 4 cups whole milk
- 1 cup unsalted butter
- 1 cup all-purpose flour
- Salt and nutmeg to taste
- 4 large eggs, beaten
- 1 cup grated Parmesan or Kefalotyri cheese

Instructions:

For the Eggplant Layer:

    Slice and Salt Eggplant:
- Slice the eggplants thinly and sprinkle salt over the slices. Let them sit for about 30 minutes to draw out moisture.

    Rinse and Pat Dry:
- Rinse the salted eggplant slices and pat them dry with paper towels.

    Grill or Roast Eggplant:

- Brush the eggplant slices with olive oil and grill or roast them until they are tender and have a golden color.

For the Meat Filling:

Cook Ground Meat:
- In a large skillet, cook the ground lamb or beef over medium heat until browned. Drain any excess fat.

Add Onions and Garlic:
- Add finely chopped onions and minced garlic to the skillet. Sauté until the onions are softened.

Add Tomato Products and Spices:
- Stir in crushed tomatoes, tomato paste, dried oregano, ground cinnamon, salt, and black pepper. Simmer until the mixture thickens. Remove from heat.

For the Béchamel Sauce:

Prepare Béchamel Sauce:
- In a saucepan, melt butter over medium heat. Add flour and whisk continuously to create a roux. Gradually pour in the milk, whisking constantly to avoid lumps.

Season and Thicken:
- Season the sauce with salt and nutmeg. Continue cooking and whisking until the béchamel thickens.

Temper Eggs:
- In a bowl, beat the eggs. Gradually add a small amount of the hot béchamel to the beaten eggs while whisking continuously (tempering the eggs).

Combine Eggs and Béchamel:
- Pour the tempered egg mixture back into the saucepan with the remaining béchamel, whisking constantly.

Add Cheese:
- Stir in the grated Parmesan or Kefalotyri cheese. Continue whisking until the sauce is smooth.

Assembling and Baking:

Layer Moussaka:

- Preheat your oven to 375°F (190°C). In a baking dish, layer half of the grilled or roasted eggplant slices. Top with the meat filling, and then layer the remaining eggplant slices.

Pour Béchamel Sauce:
- Pour the béchamel sauce over the top layer, ensuring it covers the entire surface.

Bake:
- Bake in the preheated oven for about 45-60 minutes or until the top is golden brown and the moussaka is cooked through.

Rest:
- Allow the moussaka to rest for about 15-20 minutes before slicing and serving.

Serve Warm:
- Slice and serve the Greek Moussaka warm. It pairs well with a side salad or crusty bread.

This Greek Moussaka recipe may take a bit of time, but the result is a flavorful and comforting dish that's worth the effort. Enjoy this classic Greek favorite!

Tandoori Chicken Pizza

Ingredients:

For the Tandoori Chicken:

- 1 pound boneless, skinless chicken thighs or breasts, cut into bite-sized pieces
- 1 cup plain yogurt
- 2 tablespoons Tandoori spice blend
- 1 tablespoon ginger-garlic paste
- 1 tablespoon lemon juice
- 1 teaspoon ground cumin
- 1 teaspoon ground coriander
- 1 teaspoon paprika
- Salt and black pepper to taste

For the Pizza:

- Pizza dough (store-bought or homemade)
- Olive oil for brushing
- 1 cup tomato sauce or pizza sauce
- 2 cups shredded mozzarella cheese
- 1 red onion, thinly sliced
- 1 bell pepper, thinly sliced
- Fresh cilantro, chopped (for garnish)
- Lemon wedges (for serving)

Instructions:

For the Tandoori Chicken:

Marinate Chicken:
- In a bowl, combine yogurt, Tandoori spice blend, ginger-garlic paste, lemon juice, ground cumin, ground coriander, paprika, salt, and black pepper. Mix well.

Coat Chicken:
- Add the chicken pieces to the marinade, ensuring each piece is well coated. Cover the bowl and let it marinate in the refrigerator for at least 2 hours, or preferably overnight.

Cook Chicken:

- Preheat the oven to 425°F (220°C). Place the marinated chicken on a baking sheet and bake for about 20-25 minutes or until the chicken is cooked through and slightly charred.

For the Pizza:

Preheat Oven:
- Preheat your oven according to the pizza dough instructions or around 450°F (230°C).

Roll Out Pizza Dough:
- Roll out the pizza dough on a floured surface to your desired thickness.

Assemble Pizza:
- Place the rolled-out dough on a pizza stone or baking sheet. Brush the dough with olive oil. Spread tomato sauce over the dough, leaving a border for the crust.

Add Tandoori Chicken:
- Distribute the cooked Tandoori chicken over the sauce.

Top with Vegetables and Cheese:
- Scatter sliced red onion and bell pepper over the chicken. Sprinkle shredded mozzarella cheese evenly over the top.

Bake:
- Bake in the preheated oven for about 12-15 minutes or until the crust is golden and the cheese is melted and bubbly.

Garnish and Serve:
- Remove the pizza from the oven and sprinkle chopped fresh cilantro over the top. Serve slices of Tandoori Chicken Pizza with lemon wedges on the side.

Enjoy the delightful fusion of Tandoori flavors and pizza goodness with this Tandoori Chicken Pizza. It's a creative and delicious twist on the traditional pizza.

Italian Sausage and Peppers Calzone

Ingredients:

For the Filling:

- 1 pound Italian sausage, casings removed
- 1 onion, thinly sliced
- 1 bell pepper, thinly sliced (use a mix of colors for visual appeal)
- 2 cloves garlic, minced
- 1 teaspoon dried oregano
- Salt and black pepper to taste
- Olive oil for sautéing

For the Calzone Dough:

- Pizza dough (store-bought or homemade)
- Cornmeal or flour for dusting
- Olive oil for brushing

For Assembly:

- 2 cups shredded mozzarella cheese
- 1/2 cup grated Parmesan cheese
- Marinara sauce (for dipping, optional)

Instructions:

For the Filling:

Cook Italian Sausage:
- In a skillet over medium heat, cook the Italian sausage, breaking it into crumbles, until browned and cooked through. Remove excess fat if needed.

Sauté Vegetables:
- In the same skillet, add a bit of olive oil if necessary. Sauté the sliced onion, bell pepper, and minced garlic until the vegetables are softened.

Season and Combine:
- Season the mixture with dried oregano, salt, and black pepper. Stir well to combine the flavors. Remove from heat and let the filling cool.

For the Calzone Dough:

Preheat Oven:
- Preheat your oven according to the pizza dough instructions or around 450°F (230°C).

Roll Out Dough:
- Roll out the pizza dough on a floured surface. You can divide the dough into individual portions for smaller calzones or use the entire piece for a larger one.

Add Filling and Cheese:
- Place a portion of the sausage and pepper filling on one half of the rolled-out dough. Sprinkle shredded mozzarella and grated Parmesan over the filling.

Fold and Seal:
- Fold the other half of the dough over the filling to create a half-moon shape. Press the edges to seal the calzone.

Cut Slits:
- Use a sharp knife to make a few slits on the top of the calzone to allow steam to escape during baking.

Transfer to Baking Sheet:
- Transfer the calzone to a baking sheet dusted with cornmeal or flour.

Brush with Olive Oil:
- Brush the top of the calzone with olive oil for a golden finish.

Bake:
- Bake in the preheated oven for about 15-20 minutes or until the calzone is golden brown and the dough is cooked through.

Cool and Serve:
- Allow the Italian Sausage and Peppers Calzone to cool for a few minutes before slicing. Serve warm with marinara sauce for dipping if desired.

Enjoy this Italian Sausage and Peppers Calzone as a delicious and satisfying meal. It's a great option for a casual dinner or game day snack.

Bacon-Wrapped Meatloaf

Ingredients:

For the Meatloaf:

- 1.5 pounds ground beef
- 1 cup breadcrumbs
- 1 onion, finely chopped
- 2 cloves garlic, minced
- 2 large eggs
- 1/2 cup milk
- 1/4 cup ketchup
- 2 tablespoons Worcestershire sauce
- 1 teaspoon dried thyme
- 1 teaspoon dried rosemary
- Salt and black pepper to taste

For Wrapping:

- 8-10 slices of bacon

For Glaze:

- 1/4 cup ketchup
- 2 tablespoons brown sugar
- 1 tablespoon Dijon mustard

Instructions:

For the Meatloaf:

   Preheat Oven:
   - Preheat your oven to 375°F (190°C).

   Prepare Meatloaf Mixture:
   - In a large mixing bowl, combine ground beef, breadcrumbs, chopped onion, minced garlic, eggs, milk, ketchup, Worcestershire sauce, dried thyme, dried rosemary, salt, and black pepper. Mix until well combined.

   Shape Meatloaf:
   - Transfer the meat mixture to a greased or parchment-lined baking sheet. Shape it into a loaf.

For Wrapping:

Wrap with Bacon:
- Lay slices of bacon over the top of the meatloaf, slightly overlapping each slice. Tuck the ends under the meatloaf.

For Glaze:

Prepare Glaze:
- In a small bowl, whisk together ketchup, brown sugar, and Dijon mustard to create the glaze.

Apply Glaze:
- Brush the glaze over the bacon-wrapped meatloaf, ensuring it covers the entire surface.

Baking:

Bake:
- Bake in the preheated oven for about 45-55 minutes or until the internal temperature reaches 160°F (71°C) and the bacon is crispy.

Broil for Crispy Bacon (Optional):
- If the bacon needs more crisping, you can broil the meatloaf for a few minutes, keeping a close eye to prevent burning.

Rest:
- Allow the bacon-wrapped meatloaf to rest for about 10 minutes before slicing.

Slice and Serve:
- Slice the Bacon-Wrapped Meatloaf and serve warm.

Enjoy this Bacon-Wrapped Meatloaf with your favorite side dishes. The bacon adds a smoky and savory element, making this meatloaf extra delicious. It's a perfect comfort food option for a family dinner.

Meaty Baked Ziti

Ingredients:

For the Meat Sauce:

- 1 pound ground beef or Italian sausage
- 1 onion, finely chopped
- 2 cloves garlic, minced
- 1 can (28 oz) crushed tomatoes
- 1 can (15 oz) tomato sauce
- 2 teaspoons dried oregano
- 1 teaspoon dried basil
- Salt and black pepper to taste

For the Baked Ziti:

- 1 pound ziti pasta
- 2 cups shredded mozzarella cheese
- 1 cup grated Parmesan cheese
- 1 cup ricotta cheese
- Fresh basil or parsley for garnish (optional)

Instructions:

For the Meat Sauce:

Cook Meat:
- In a large skillet over medium heat, cook the ground beef or Italian sausage until browned. Drain any excess fat.

Sauté Onion and Garlic:
- Add finely chopped onion and minced garlic to the skillet. Sauté until the onion is softened.

Add Tomato Products and Seasonings:
- Stir in crushed tomatoes, tomato sauce, dried oregano, dried basil, salt, and black pepper. Simmer the sauce for about 15-20 minutes to allow the flavors to meld. Remove from heat.

For the Baked Ziti:

Preheat Oven:
- Preheat your oven to 375°F (190°C).

Cook Ziti:

- Cook the ziti pasta according to package instructions until al dente. Drain and set aside.

Combine Pasta and Sauce:
- In a large mixing bowl, combine the cooked ziti with the meat sauce. Mix until the pasta is evenly coated with the sauce.

Layer in Baking Dish:
- In a greased or parchment-lined baking dish, layer half of the ziti and sauce mixture. Dollop half of the ricotta cheese over the pasta. Sprinkle half of the shredded mozzarella and grated Parmesan over the top. Repeat the layers with the remaining ziti and cheeses.

Bake:
- Bake in the preheated oven for about 25-30 minutes or until the cheese is melted and bubbly.

Broil for Golden Top (Optional):
- If you want a golden-brown top, you can broil the baked ziti for a few minutes, keeping a close eye to prevent burning.

Garnish and Serve:
- Remove the baked ziti from the oven. Garnish with fresh basil or parsley if desired. Allow it to cool for a few minutes before serving.

Serve Warm:
- Scoop out portions of Meaty Baked Ziti and serve warm.

Enjoy this Meaty Baked Ziti with a side of garlic bread or a green salad for a satisfying and comforting meal. It's a perfect dish for gatherings and family dinners.

www.ingramcontent.com/pod-product-compliance
Lightning Source LLC
LaVergne TN
LVHW081550060526
838201LV00054B/1840